The Mission to
END SLAVERY

What if Slavery Never Existed?

**Denis Olasehinde
Akinmolasire**

The Mission to End Slavery

Denis Olasehinde Akinmolasire

AKINSTER BOOKS

Contents

About the Author

Denis Olasehinde Akinmolasire is a software engineer who has always enjoyed writing.

Following on from his first book *Love, War and Glory: Spoken Words for All Seasons*, he is now sharing his debut novel with the world under his own publishing label, Akinster Books.

Denis is hoping his book *The Mission to End Slavery* will make people think about what the world would have been like if slavery had never occurred.

Additionally his book covers what the key events were that led to slavery becoming a nightmare and reality for the world.

Acknowledgements

December 2017; this is when my journey to becoming an author began. I was sitting at home reading some of my old writings that were on my laptop and I said to myself, 'Why don't you write a book?' Two years later, Book 2 and my own publishing label, Akinster Books, is upon us.

These journeys do not happen without good people being around us. First of all I would like to thank my family – my mum and sisters especially – who have always supported me in terms of the path I have taken in life.

I would like to thank at this time of writing my wife-to-be, Stacey, whose love and kindness has helped guide me on this journey. Love you always, xxx.

I would like to thank my friends in my WhatsApp groups, especially Ay-rab Money, Garage Event and Manchester United, who have always had my back in good times and bad, and were very supportive when my first book launched.

I also would like to express thanks to my colleagues at work. When they heard that I had written a book they were all excited and told me off for not sharing the news with them earlier. Everyone at work has always been behind me, even in my bad moments.

Lastly I want to thank you, my reader, for taking the time to read this book. Without our readers, us authors wouldn't have an audience to tell our stories to. I want to thank you all for showing your support. I have no idea where the writing journey is going to lead to, but I hope you will continue to enjoy my books. So for now please sit back, relax with your favourite beverage(s) and enjoy the story.

Thanks always,

Denis Olasehinde Akinmolasire
Founder of Akinster Books

What's it all about?

'**Slavery**; the practice and system of owning slaves. It is a condition of having to work very hard without being properly remunerated or appreciated', that's a dictionary definition of slavery.

In reality it means something much worse. Slavery can be equated with cruelty, oppression, suffering, discrimination and being treated as a lesser human being. For the most part in the world today slavery has been abolished. Yet in the world we live in today we still see people suffering. Human trafficking takes place on a daily basis; many people are underpaid and undervalued, and live in terrible conditions. The peoples of Africa and the Caribbean have never been compensated for the horrors their ancestors suffered centuries ago. I often ask myself what it would take to eliminate slavery.

What would the world be like if slavery had never existed? What was the root cause of slavery? And this is where my story begins.

This is for real!

Deep into the night Femi was woken up by a noise. He went out and looked around but he couldn't see anything. He tried to go back to sleep, but he heard the noise again. This time it was a little louder. He got up again. The noise was followed by a roar.

Femi prodded Chief Oko: 'Chief, wake up.'

'What is it, Femi?'

'There's something there.'

'What *is* it?' Chief Oko asked, yawning.

'Just listen.'

They went outside and a few moments later the roar came again.

'Femi, grab our weapons.'

Femi dashed back in to fetch them. Alert to the approaching danger, Chief Oko, on receiving his sword, spear and shield, took his battle stance.

'Prepare yourself,' he warned Femi.

'What's out there?' Femi asked.

'A beast,' Chief Oko replied grimly.

A few moments later they heard another roar. Chief Oko and Femi turned their backs to each other to give them the best possible view of the threat while protecting their backs.

They heard a faint padding. The padding got closer and closer. Then a figure emerged from the shadows. It was a lion. But the lion was not alone. Two more lions emerged – they closed in and began to circle around Chief Oko and Femi in anticipation of their next meal.

'Errr, is this part of the training you've been giving me?' Femi asked, tongue in cheek.

'No, this is for real! If you fall here you die. No repeat.'

Chapter 1: The cost of slavery

Our tale begins in East Ham, East London, on 16th March 2019. Femi Adebayo was returning home from St Bonaventure's Sixth Form.

He visited his local barbershop, often seen as one of the cornerstones of the black community. The barbershop is not just a place where people come to have their hair cut. It also acts as a social gathering place where people can express their feelings without fear of prejudice, and be amongst other people that will have a better understanding of where they are coming from. The barbershop often throws up conversations that have a deep meaning within the community. This was especially true of Femi's visit that day.

'Yo, Femi, what's up?' asked Akinjade. '

'I'm well,' Femi replied.

'Take a seat, Femi; I'll be with you when I can.' Akinjade was the owner of the barbershop. His family had owned it for two decades, and he had taken it over when his father had retired and decided to head home to Nigeria.

'Akinjade,' said one of the customers, 'is it possible to change the channel? The match has finished'.

'Sure thing; let me see what else is on.' After flicking through the channels, Akinjade stumbled across a special news feature on BBC One.

The programme in question was looking at the role of black sports stars and their impact on the UK. Initially everyone in the barbershop carried on with what they were doing. Then a reporter made a comment which made them sit up and take notice.

The reporter said, 'Personally, I feel like these guys don't take their positions as role models seriously enough. I mean, look at Raheem Sterling; why does he feel the need to go out and get a gun tattoo? Or Paul Pogba, what's with all the changing of haircuts every week?' A silence echoed around the barbershop. Everyone stopped what they doing, turned their attention to the TV, and stared at the screen until the programme finished. They looked at each other with disgust and anger at what they had just watched.

'What kind of bullshit programming is *that*?' one of Akinjade's customers said.

'How on earth is the BBC allowed to put on shit like this?' yelled another. 'Seriously, *that's* what we spend our licence fee on?'

Femi nodded in agreement with the comments. 'What do you expect? This is the world we live in. They make the rules, not us.'

'You know what? This is one of the things that really pisses me off about this country and the western world in general,' growled Akinjade. 'Why is it they're always trying to take black people down a peg? I mean, seriously, they're having a go at Raheem Sterling for buying his mum a house. But when Phil Forden does it – a *white* footballer, might I add – he gets praised and is seen as a good guy. They often can't stand it when a black person is successful.'

'I couldn't agree with you more,' said Tokunbo. He had been a barber in the shop for many years and he had often spoken out against black discrimination. 'It's as if it's one rule for them and another for us. I mean, just look at Ashley Cole – look at all the rubbish he gets because he cheated on Cheryl Cole. Now I'm a Manchester United supporter, and loved them as players because they served our club well – but David Beckham had a fling with Rebecca Loos during his time at Real Madrid and he's still a worldwide icon. Ryan Giggs had an affair with his brother's wife; that's adultery and betraying a family member, yet I'm still seeing him on ITV providing commentary for international matches and he gets the Wales job. I mean, seriously, what's up with that?'

'It's true,' Akinjade nodded in agreement.

'Speaking of managers,' Tokunbo went on, 'why is it when an internationally renowned white football player goes into management they often go in at the top end? I mean, just look at Steven

Gerrard at Glasgow Rangers and Frank Lampard at Derby. Whereas someone like Soul Campbell – who I might add was in the team of the tournament at the 2002 World Cup and was arguably one of the best defenders in Europe if not the world during his prime – *he* has to start at Macclesfield in Division Two. Heh, Steven Gerrard and Frank Lampard were badman footballers back in the day, but c'mon now; everyone can see that this isn't right. Gary Neville went straight from the Sky pundits chair to his Valencia job. Does he even know a word of Spanish? I mean, *please.*

'*And,*' he continued, 'don't even get me started on how they treat drug cheats. Even though they eventually caught Lance Armstrong there's no way he suffered as much as Ben Johnson did. Lance is still filthy rich, whereas Ben struggled to make a living after his athletics career was done. Or if we take a look closer to home, just look at how Dwayne Chambers has been treated. He did wrong, but anyone would think he'd committed murder the way people carry on. Why is it any time he's introduced they always say *Dwayne Chambers, the former drugs cheat*? Why is it I never hear Maria Sharapova, Marin Cilic or Shane Warne, the cricket player, ever introduced as former drugs cheats? Cilic even came back and won a grand slam, and no one batted an eyelid. Even Andre Agassi, when he was going through his slump in 1997 and failed a drugs test – they just swept it underneath the carpet, and when he came back and started winning grand slams he got away with it scot free! If he'd been black, do you think that would have happened? Not a chance in hell!'

'Hear, hear!' said everyone in the barbershop.

Tokunbo finished cutting his client's hair and put down his trimmer. He turned to everyone in the barbershop: 'Why is it when someone speaks out about these things they always manage to find a way to shut us up or take us down? History has shown that. Martin Luther King, he had a dream. They killed him to stop that dream from becoming a reality. Malcolm X, the same thing. I mean, let's look at the 1968 Olympics when those two American athletes did the black power salute. Guess what happened to them? They never competed at another Olympics. It's basically if you're not with the system you're against it.'

Akinjade responded, 'And let's not forget Jesse Owens, who went to the 1936 Olympics in Berlin and won four gold medals, sticking two fingers up at Hitler and the Nazis – yet when he headed back to the USA he couldn't find any work. He had to race against horses to make a living. What kind of nonsense is that? Can you imagine that happening to Usain Bolt? No way would that be happening. It would create a riot.'

Tokunbo interjected, 'True, but Usain Bolt is accepted by the masses. When they accept you or see you as one of their own they'll treat you very differently. Case in point, Frank Bruno or Lenny Henry in comparison to say Lennox Lewis or Doc

Brown. Sometimes it isn't about whether you're actually good at what you do. It's all this other nonsense that can make or break you. That shows you the kind of world we live in.'

Tokunbo continued on his stance: 'When they need you they'll treat you like gold. When they don't need you they'll cast you out like a leper. I mean, check this out.' Tokunbo reached into his pocket and pulled out his phone. 'There's an article from that stupid newspaper called *The Sun* that I want to show you all.'

'You read *The Sun,* Tokunbo?' said Akinjade. 'Man, you know you can't take that paper seriously. That paper's always chatting wet.'

'True, that, Akinjade. But their football stuff's mostly on point. You know me – I read my newspapers back to front. But anyway, check this out; there was an article sent to me on WhatsApp that you mans need to read. Here we go – look at this! Look at how they're disrespecting Mo Farah. This is what *The Sun*'s writing on 27th April 2019. Here's their exact words ... *The Olympic hero's remarkable capacity to win medals and break records for Team GB can be equally matched by an aptitude to attract the wrong type of headlines.* You see this? It gets better. They go on to state how before the 2012 Olympics he missed a drugs test because he couldn't hear them ringing the bell. Then they say that the drug testers were waiting nearly an hour for them. I mean, how do they know if he was actually in? Maybe he was out in the garden or something.'

Akinjade reminded everyone in the shop that people had been sceptical about athletics for years: 'Heh, we got to be careful when it comes to athletics. Just remember the Balco scandal.'

Tokunbo acknowledged Akinjade's point, but he went on to question the timing of the article. 'Athletics is unfortunately quite a dirty sport these days, Akinjade, and you know I love my sprinting. But let's rewind this and get back to the matter at hand here. Why is it they're only printing this now? It's 2019, and this incident happened, what, seven years ago. Doesn't that seem odd to you? When Mo Farah was winning gold medals left right and centre at the Olympics and World Championships, no one said anything. Why is it that the moment he stops track running and pretty much retires from an Olympics perspective, they suddenly want to start chatting their lyrics? The moment there's no gold medal in it for them – no *more*, that is – is when they want to try and tear him down. Let's not forget if it weren't for Mo Farah at the London World Championships in 2017 they wouldn't have won a single individual gold medal. Take away the relays, and if it weren't for Mo Farah they wouldn't have won shit. I find it wrong that they don't write about how all their other athletes failed to deliver at a home world athletics championship. I mean, what kind of dumb arse double standards is this? Explain that one to me.'

'The media plays a huge role in how black people are viewed in this country, unfortunately,' Akinjade said. 'If the media thinks you're great then everyone'll think you're great. If the media thinks you're crap they'll do everything possible in their power to make sure that everybody else thinks you're crap as well. I swear we need a national newspaper that defends the right of black people.'

He continued, 'We need to get our views represented at national level. We need more blacks in the media to counteract a lot of the institutionalised racism and propaganda that exists.'

'We've got to give our youths examples for them to look up to. They're the generation that's going to make the difference. Once we start breaking into these circles then we'll start seeing changes. It only takes one man to make a difference. The challenge is, we still have all these brick walls that are blocking our path to progress.'

During this debate Femi had remained very quiet, paying close attention to what was being said. Femi always enjoyed these debates; he found he came away from them with new knowledge and perspectives. Very often he would be in agreement with what was being discussed, as he had often already held the same views himself.

Femi interjected, 'Here's the thing I don't get. Why is it in 2019 we're still talking about race? I mean, we've been on these shores for hundreds of years, yet in a lot of cases we're still treated as second-class citizens. How can a party like the BNP exist, with people like Nick Clegg effectively telling us to fuck off and go back to where we come from? If that was the Black Man's Party preaching similar stuff it'd be outlawed straight away. The question I have is what's the root of all of this? I mean all the things we've been discussing are just the symptoms. They're not the root cause of the issue. What's the actual problem that we need to tackle?'

'That's an easy one to solve, Femi,' Tokunbo responded. 'The issue's society, innit? Society needs to changed. They don't understand us. Not language wise, but culturally. They don't get our style, the way we think or work. And worse, they don't understand what's important to us. If you look at institutions such as the police, how many black people do they have working in that area? Look at the newspapers that we read – *The Sun*, *Daily Mirror*, *Independent*, *Metro*, *Evening Standard*. I mean, look at the writers behind each article. Where are they from? OK, so we have newspapers like *The Voice,* but outside of certain boroughs in London is that as well known as it should be? If we look at other industries and start digging into the organisations at some of the biggest companies in the world, how many of their CEOs, CIOs and all the other people in charge are from black and other ethnic minorities? If the people in power don't share the same background and culture as our own, can we realistically expect them to understand where we're coming from?'

'Agreed!' shouted the people in the shop.

'Those things you're talking about, Tokunbo, are related to recruitment, though. Where are these companies going to get their employees from? Are they coming into inner city schools? Are they visiting all the different African and Caribbean societies at every university? For some of those professions that they're looking at, do black people even consider those professions? In Nigeria the big professions are accounting, doctoring and – because of the oil companies – chemical engineering. When it comes to our parents' generation, if you mention a field such as computer science, I guarantee you that they'll look back at you and say *Ah, eh, you cannot take that course, oh. Go back and fill in that application form again, jor.*'

Everyone in the barber shop laughed at Femi's comments in his fake Nigerian accent, as they could all relate to what he was saying.

Femi continued to express his views: 'The mentality of our parent's generation is a hurdle, too, as when our parents came over here they didn't have some of the opportunities that exist now. So they can't be blamed for that. I feel there's more to the problem. There's something else causing all these issues. But I'm struggling to think what that is.'

'I think I know the answer, Femi,' said Akinjade. 'But to understand it we have to go way back. I mean back to the time of civilisations such as the Romans. You want to know what our real problem is? When you break it down, it all comes down to one thing: slavery.'

'Slavery?' the people in the shop shouted.

'Yes, slavery.'

One customer responded, 'But slavery happened thousands of years ago, Akinjade.'

'True, but we're still suffering from it. Let's break it all down, shall we? What happened during slavery? We had black people getting treated as second-class citizens. Does that still go on today? Yep! Do we still have black people getting raped and murdered for no good reason? You bet your arse we do. How many times have the police stopped us and beaten us up without just cause? Look at how the western world took all of our natural resources without paying us a fair price for them. The western world has been taking resources such as gold, oil and rice from the motherland for years. What did we get in return? A third-world debt imposed on us by – you guessed it – western countries. If that's not *Ole* [Yoruba for 'thief'] I don't know what is. I mean, c'mon, but what is this bullshit? Slavery still exists. It's just the form of how slavery is imposed on us is different.' Akinjade kissed his teeth at an unjust world.

Femi said: 'Akinjade, you're not wrong, bro. But here's the thing. It's all well and good identifying what the problem is – but we can't change what happened in the past. So the question is how do we move forward?'

'Good question, Femi. Firstly we need education. We need to educate our people on what's really going on and what happened. How many of you have ever wondered how the British Empire came to be? Here's how the British themselves conquered and divided us. People often think that the history of slavery lies in countries such as the USA; wrong. Wrong. The British have as much blood on their hands as anybody. In 1562 Captain John Hawkins went to West Africa and started capturing people and selling them to white people in the Caribbean as slaves. By 1730 Britain was the biggest slave trader in the world. Go to Bristol. You can find all the slave reports there. In 1760 came the first major protest, led by a slave called Tacky. But Tacky was captured and beheaded. How many times have we heard that story before, hmmm?'

'Britain had the most slaves in the world at one point?' said a very surprised Femi.

Akinjade, nodding, added, 'But the national curriculum doesn't teach you that. Instead they go and teach you about that greedy fat kunt Henry the Eighth having six wives and all that crap. They don't teach you about the *real* history. They don't teach you about what's really up. Eric Killmonger in Black Panther had a point. Certain punks need to pay for this injustice.'

Femi was a little startled at Akinjade's sudden bloodlust: 'Don't you think that's a little extreme? I mean Eric Killmonger wanted to send out weapons to kill basically whoever stood in the way of our community. The problem with an eye for an eye is that everyone ends up blind.'

Akinjade responded, 'Maybe it's a little extreme. But,' he added passionately, 'the west needs to man up and own up to its sins. We need a real apology from those people. They need to pay back what they stole. They need to pay back our resources and our time, but more importantly our freedom.'

Tokunbo walked up to Akinjade and sympathetically placed a hand on his right shoulder. 'Heh, look, Akinjade, everyone in the shop hears you and feels your pain. But the government isn't going to apologise for what's happened. That isn't realistic. Slavery has set us back hundreds of years. This isn't something we can fix just like that. It's going to take a lot of time. To be frank, the solution will probably not even come in our lifetime.'

Deep down, Akinjade knew Tokunbo was right: 'It's true, Tokunbo, but we have to do our bit. We have to spread this knowledge. We have to help each other out. Sometimes we're our own worst enemy. Out of all the races, sometimes I feel like we're the most divided. Instead of helping each other out we are often fighting each other and give each other screw face looks. I mean, why? Why do we do that to each other? Mario Balotelli asked the question 'Why always me?' – but the question should really be Why always *us*? We already have the world against us – why do we need to turn on each other as well? If we aren't united, what chance do we stand? Anyway, excuse my boldness. You know what I'm like. Sometimes I just want to run down the street and say to the world, *Screw you, I'm doing things my way!* Unfortunately if I did that I'd probably end up being arrested for disorderly behaviour – and where would that get me? I can't help anyone if I'm locked away.'

Femi analysed what Akinjade was saying, and was keen to draw out some conclusions: 'If I've understood what you're saying, you think we need education, we need the west to apologise and to return what they have stolen from us, and we need to unite ourselves. These things make sense, especially in the long term, but what I'd really like to know is what we can we do in the here and now? I mean, I won't be around in 100 years. Do we really need to wait that long before we can see progress?'

'We need a revolution, Femi. But these things, like it or not, are going to take time. They don't happen overnight,' Tokunbo responded. 'The amount of damage that's been done to the Black Community is so deep-rooted it has manifested itself into all areas of society. This is the point that Akinjade, I think, is getting at. We need a massive cleanup and clearout of the dirt that's engulfed this world. Only when that's done do we stand a chance. To be frank, we need blood and sweat to be spilled.'

At that point Akinjade, having finished with his current customer, said, 'Femi, it's your turn to get a shape-up.'

Femi walked over to Akinjade's chair. When Akinjade was finished Femi gave him £7 to pay for his haircut and said to him, 'Akinjade, I know the world's messed up, man, but someday it's going to be fixed. I just feel that that we won't be around to see that happen. Until then we have to keep soldiering on.'

'I know, bro. See you soon, Femi.'

Femi left the barbershop and began making his way home. On the way, he kept thinking back to the discussion that had just occurred, and he looked back at what he had witnessed in his own life.

'They're right. This all started with slavery,' he thought to himself. 'If it weren't for slavery, the world would be a much better place.' He continued his journey home. As he was walking past an alleyway on Barking Road he suddenly heard a bottle break. He turned around but he couldn't see anything – and then he heard another bottle break …

'Who's there?' he asked. He decided to walk down the alleyway in case something was wrong and there was someone that needed help.

'Hello. Is anyone here?' he asked as he reached the end of the alleyway.

And he heard a voice: 'Interesting views in the barbershop you had back there, young man.'

Femi looked around but he couldn't see anyone. 'Who said that? Who are you? Show yourself.'

A mysterious man walked out of the shadows. He wore shades and had a silky-smooth pose and an aura about him, almost like a modern-day Shaft. But Femi just thought he looked like a high-class pimp rolling in cash.

'I couldn't help but overhear the interesting discussion you just had in the barbershop, said the man. 'Are you free to discuss it some more?'

'That depends. Are you stalking me?' asked Femi with his arms crossed.

The man sensed Femi's distrust. 'My apologies, I didn't mean to startle you. I was just walking past the barbershop earlier and I found it a fascinating conversation. The conclusion that slavery is at the root of all the problems that we have in the world today I find provocative at the very least. It's true what they say; you can find the most interesting debates in barbershops.'

'Interesting debate, huh! You still haven't told me who you are,' Femi repeated.

'Oh, sorry. My sincere apologies, young man. How rude of me. My name's Mr Diggity. I'm here to talk you about an initiative I'd like you to be a part of. It's called the Mission to End Slavery.'

Chapter 2: Meet Mr Diggity

'*The Mission to End Slavery?* OK, let's slow down for a second. I mean, you just popped out of nowhere. So where did you come from?' Femi asked.

'Where I'm from doesn't matter. What matters, Femi, is what I can offer you.'

Femi warily asked, 'How do you know my name?'

'How I know your name? As a certain famous wrestler used to say ... it doesn't matter how I know your name. Sorry, I've always wanted to do that.' The man just stood there before Femi and started giggling to himself.

'I don't have time for this,' Femi said before turning round and continuing his walk.

'What's your hurry? I thought you wanted to moan and bitch about how bad the world is.'

Femi paused, then slowly turned around and asked, 'Remind me what your name is again?'

'Mr Diggity. I've been watching you for a while, Femi.'

'Watching me? So you *are* a stalker!' Femi responded.

'No,' said Mr Diggity. 'You may think of me as a talent spotter. Let's just say I'm always on the lookout for talented individuals who aren't fulfilling their potential.'

Femi stood there in amusement. 'Really? I'm on my way to getting three As at A Level. I've got interviews lined up with some of the best universities in the country – Imperial, Loughborough and Durham. I have my whole life ahead of me. So just you tell me how I'm not fulfilling my potential.'

Mr Diggity calmly walked up to him and smiled. He pointed at Femi's heart and said to him: 'You're unfulfilled *here*.'

Curious, Femi said, 'How do you mean?'

Mr Diggity asked. 'Tell me, Femi, are you happy? I mean really happy?'

Femi responded. 'Yes! I mean, why do you ask me that?'

'So you're happy? Hmmm,' Mr Diggity said unconvinced. 'Then tell me, why do you have such a big chip on your shoulder? Why do you always walk around looking like you're ready to fight? It's as if you're always on guard, watching over your shoulder. Never allowing yourself to truly rest and be happy. You say you have all these opportunities and a bright future to look forward to, yet you're always seeking something else. If you're truly happy, why aren't you enjoying life?'

Femi, a bit annoyed, said, 'Look, I don't know you and you don't know me. You don't know *anything* about me.'

'Denial … why do they always deny it when they're confronted with the truth?' Mr Diggity said to the air.

'Truth, what truth?' Femi asked.

'You tell me, Femi; what's really on your mind? Look at what you were just saying in the barbershop. All that animosity, all that anguish, all that pain. You try to keep a straight face, you try to be strong for your mum and your sisters – but deep down you know the truth.'

'Don't mention my family again, you prick,' Femi snapped.

'Why? Did I hit a nerve?' Mr Diggity smirked.

Femi, staring at him straight in the face, said, 'What do you want?'

Mr Diggity said, 'Simple, I want you to tell me the truth. What's really on your mind?'

Femi shoved him, saying, 'All right, you *really* want to know what I think? I'm sick and fed up of having to work twice as hard because I'm black. I'm sick and fed up of being considered to be in a minority. I'm sick and tired of any crime or bad thing that happens in this world being prefixed with the word *black*. It's as if anything viewed with black is instantly seen as bad. Whenever a knife crime takes place, it always gets associated with black people somehow. Whenever there is underachievement in certain boroughs of London, look at how they always talk about the black kids. The only time the news will mention anything about Africa is when there's a disaster. They're always quick to mention 619-type situations or corruption, yet the west's just as corrupt as anywhere else. Sepp Blatter and all the shady inner workings of FIFA, Brexit, Monica Lewinsky getting it on with Bill Clinton in comparison – all these things get swept underneath the carpet. And as for sport, they love us when we're performing for them, but the moment we aren't we're treated like second-class citizens. Dwayne Chambers, for instance, has been victimised over the drug situation, and every time he competes he's introduced as a former drugs cheat. Maria Sharapova, Marin Cilic and Shane Warne, as you heard in the shop, have had drug bans – but none of them has ever been introduced as a former drugs cheat. Alan Wells was proved to be a drugs cheat, but nothing gets said about him, either. If you go into the cinema, how many times in a film is the black person always the first to die? Even in Avengers Infinity War, Heimdall dies after five minutes. That's *Idris Elba*, for crying out loud! I love the Marvel films but that really pissed me off. And then Western films nearly always project Indians as the bad guys and the whites as the good guys, whereas historically Indians were peaceful people. To put it simply I'm getting fed up of one rule for them and another rule for everybody else.'

Femi paused for a moment to get his breath back.

Mr Diggity looked up at him and applauded: 'Bravo! A man who's not afraid to speak what's on his mind. I respect that immensely. But let me ask you something. Do you think that you're the only ones who have suffered? Don't you think people of other colours and races haven't suffered as well?'

Femi responded, 'Yes, of course they have – but none have had it as bad as us.'

'Really?' Mr Diggity said calmly as he raised his eyebrows and lowered his sunglasses. 'Let's have a history lesson, shall we? Take the Arab invaders of Sind in the 8th century and the armies of the Umayyad commander Muhammad bin Qasim. They went to India and enslaved thousands of Indians. Women, children, and soldiers – no one was spared. The Tang dynasty resulted in Turks, Persians, Indonesians, Mongolians, central Asians, and northern Indians amongst others, being sold into slavery. Even in the late 1990s millions of girls were bonded in Pakistan and sold into the slave trade. Slavery has affected every part of the world and not just black people.'

Femi, disgusted, said, 'Then why are *we* still paying the price for what the western world's done to us? No justice, no retribution! The western world's literally been allowed to get away with murder.

'Hey, don't shoot the messenger! I'm not disagreeing with what you're saying, at all. I'm on your side, kid. However, what I'm saying is why is it that other communities have been able to move forward but the black community hasn't. Why is it I can go to certain areas in London such as Upton Park or Chinatown and see communities of Asians, Indians and other cultures building a future or a legacy for themselves? Why can't black communities do that? Why can't I look forward to Nigerian, Ghanaian and other African restaurants serving food in areas such as Leicester Square or Westfield Stratford City? Why is it I can't go to Tottenham Court Road or Knightsbridge and order some poundered yam? You feel me? If we can have a black president of the USA, why can't we have establishments that celebrate black culture? Do you think it was slavery that stopped that from happening? If so, how come it hasn't stopped other cultures?'

Femi was stunned by Mr Diggity's response, and had to pause for a moment. He really needed to think deeply about what Mr Diggity had just said to him.

'You know what?' said Femi. 'You actually have a point. However the amount of times black people have tried to take a stand and we've been shut down, closed off or, worse still, taken out. I mean, you only have to look at have happened to people such as Martin Luther King and Malcolm X.'

'For every example you throw at me, Femi, I can throw up so many counter-examples. Richard de Zoysa and Oscar Romero spring to my mind.'

'Are you trying to dismiss the problems that our community has? Considering the colour of your skin, it's as if you don't want to defend our people.'

Mr Diggity tutted and nodded his head. He placed one arm on Femi's shoulder: 'On the contrary, Femi, all I'm trying to do is get you to be open-minded. Your heart's in the right place. But I fear that you are dramatically over-simplifying things. The way you think, it's as if all the world's problems would disappear if slavery didn't exist.'

'Of course they would,' Femi responded angrily. 'Think about it! Think about all the people that would have been saved. Think about everything that we have lost as people. Centuries ago our ancestors suffered because of cowards that brought guns. They robbed from us, stole our ideas, had a negative influence on our culture and ideas, and scattered us. Africa was never divided into large countries with straight boundaries. It was the west that came in and created all these divisions, it's thanks to them that so many of our people are in poverty today.

'And then, why is it that while most of the world can speak English the majority of us can't speak the language of our parents? In school here we learn about history, but only up to a certain point. Because if they were to go back further it would expose the truth of what happened to us. If it weren't for slavery, bastards like Alexander the Great and Napoleon would not have been able to build their empires. Their empires were built through conquering, torture and most significantly slavery. If I had the chance I'd go back in time and stop all those things from happening.'

'So, why don't you, then?' Mr Diggity said, smiling.

'Why don't I do *what*?' Femi asked.

'Why don't you go back in time and stop slavery from ever happening?' Mr Diggity asked.

Femi looked at Mr Diggity and said, 'That's impossible. Time travel doesn't exist.'

Mr Diggity said to Femi, 'Who says it doesn't?'

Femi paused for a moment, and thought to himself, 'What's this guy saying?'

'Femi, what about if I told you there was a way to stop slavery? What about if I told you that time travel is very real and very possible? What about if I offered you the chance to go back in time and change history, and stop slavery from ever coming to be?'

For a moment Femi was stunned. Then he burst into gales of laughter: 'Ha ha ha ha ha ha ha ha ha. That was a good one. What's that saying, *It's good to laugh*?'

'This is no laughing matter. I'm serious. You're the one always saying how you'd like to change the world for the better. You said you wanted to eliminate slavery. Well, sir, now's your chance. I have the means to make this a possibility.'

'Yeah, right. You're a crazy one, Mr Diggity,' came Femi's response. Then he took a look at his phone and, realising that his mum was looking to cook a new beef stew today, he picked up his bag, ready to set off on his walk home.

'Look, Mr Diggity, it was nice talking to you. You're a little bit on the crazy side, but this has been fun. I'll see you around.'

'I'll be waiting right here if you change your mind,' Mr Diggity said.

Femi smiled at him and as he left said to himself, 'Time travel, go back in time and change history. Who has time to come up with something like that?'

Chapter 3: Disaster strikes

On Saturday Femi and his little sister, Titilayo, did the weekly family shop. They headed into Sainsburys. Femi very often was the one who had to carry the shopping home; he had not passed his driving test yet. On this occasion he had managed to drag Titilayo along with him.

'I really hate these shopping trips. I have better things to do with my time,' she complained.

'Better things, like what? Comb your hair?' Femi replied.

'It takes ages to do a girl's hair. You're a guy – all you have to do is go down to the barbershop and get a 10-minute trim, and you're sorted. It isn't like that for me.'

'That may be so, but you know the weekly shopping needs to be done. It can't be just me all the time doing it.'

'But you're a man. You can lift stuff, Femi.'

'Ever heard of a trolley, Titilayo?'

'Push a trolley around here – do you know how embarrassing that is? When are you going to get your licence?'

'Soon – but what about when I'm not around, though?'

Titilayo, a little stunned, asked, 'What do you mean, not around?'

'I'm going to university next year; don't forget that. You'll need to step up and help Mum out more.'

'I know, Femi.'

'Do you though, Titi? Sometimes, Titi, I feel like you expect food to be on the table but you're not prepared to help get it or make the meals. You're not a baby any more. You're becoming an adult, and you need to start taking more ownership of the things that go on at home –cooking, cleaning, paying bills. Me and Olamide won't be at home for ever.'

'You're right, brother. I'm sorry. I didn't mean to leave you and Mum in the lurch. I guess it's just that you've all shielded me from things. Perhaps it's been because of me being the youngest, so maybe I've never felt the pressure. I mean, Olamide's the oldest and the firstborn, and you're the only boy – the golden boy I might add.'

'Golden boy? I don't think so.'

'I'm serious, Femi. Mum's always praising you. She's always telling us we should follow your example.'

'I find that very hard to believe, as she's never ever told me that in person.'

'Maybe that's her way of keeping you hungry. And you don't really do well with compliments,

Femi. You respond better when people tell you what you're *not* doing well!'

'You know me too well, Titilayo.'

'I'm your sister, so I'm supposed to.'

They smiled at each other.

'I'll miss you when you go to university, Femi.'

'I know, Titi. I'm going to miss you as well. I don't mean to nag you or have a go at you. I just need to know that you're going to be there for Mum when I'm no longer around. Mum's going to really need your support when I'm gone, and I need you to be there for her. We're lucky that our mum's a very strong woman. You as well as anyone know what our mum has had to go through since Dad died. But she's getting older. She won't be able to do everything for ever. So please, when I'm gone make sure you help her.'

'I promise, Femi. I'll be there for her always. You have my word.'

'Thank you, Titilayo. Now let's head home so that you can get back to combing your hair.'

'Shut up!' Titilayo said, laughing.

The two headed to the bus stop, but on the way a group of four men approached them. They wore masks and were covered head to toe in white clothing. It was as if the Ku Klux Klan had come to east London.

Titilayo looked at them, worried, and asked Femi, 'Who are these guys?'

'I have no idea. Let's just keep calm and carry on. We're in a public place, so they'd be foolish to try anything stupid.'

One of the men approached them. Looking at Femi he said to him, 'What have you got there?'

'Food.'

'Who for?'

'My family,' Femi said defiantly.

'Fool! Not any more – that's *my* food now.' The man tried to grab a bag from Femi.

'Heh, what are you doing, man?' said Femi.

The other men attacked him. He quickly found himself overwhelmed by the four of them.

Wishing to help her brother, Titilayo jumped in. 'Let him go!' she screamed as she tried to pull one of the men off her brother. The man lashed out at Titilayo and pushed her off him. He reached into his pocket, pulled out a knife and stabbed her in the chest. She let out a scream and the men dropped Femi.

One of the men shouted at the stabber, 'What the fuck are you doing? Let's get out of here.'

The four men ran off, leaving a helpless Femi to pick up the pieces. He slowly got back to his feet and looked up at Titilayo – and saw the blood on her left hand and her shirt.

'Titi!' screamed Femi as she collapsed.

Onlookers began to appear on the scene. Within moments Femi and Titilayo were surrounded, Femi holding his sister in his arms.

'Somebody help! Call an ambulance!' Femi shouted.

The ambulance arrived fifteen minutes later, and rushed Femi and his sister off to Newham General Hospital. She was taken straight into surgery. As Femi waited outside the theatre he was joined by his mum and Olamide.

'Femi!' Seeing him, his mum ran up and hugged him tight. She was thankful to see that at least Femi was alive and in one piece. Olamide joined in the hugging.

'Are you all right?' Femi's mum asked.

'I'm fine, Mum.'

'What happened?' Olamide asked.

'As we were heading home from Sainsburys four men dressed in white clothes attacked us. Titilayo tried to get one of them off me. In return the man stabbed her.'

'Oh my God!' Femi's mum was about to burst into tears.

Femi gave her another reassuring cuddle. 'Titi's a tough girl. She'll survive. For now all we can do is just be here for her when she wakes up.'

Femi, Olamide and his mum sat down together in the waiting room. They held each other's hands in unity to support each other and to give each other strength during this testing period.

An hour later one of the doctors emerged from the theatre. The moment they saw him, Femi, his mum and Olamide got up from their seats to hear the latest. Each of them braced themselves to hear the worst.

'The good news is the operation was successful. We've stabilised her.'

'Thank god,' the family said in relief.

'However, she's in a weak condition as a result of losing a lot of blood. We'll need to keep her in overnight to monitor her in case something changes.'

'Thank you, Doctor,' Femi's mum said. The family were able to stay overnight at the hospital. The police came by to speak to Femi, but he asked if he could speak with them tomorrow. Tonight it was about Femi being there for his family.

Chapter 4: The mission begins

A couple of days had passed since the incident. Femi had told the police everything that had happened, but he hadn't heard back from them. So Femi and Akinjade marched into East Ham police station to get an update on their investigation and to try to get justice for Femi's sister. But no real progress was being made.

'Is that it? My sister's in the hospital fighting for her life and all you can tell me is that you'll provide an update as soon as possible?' Femi shouted at the station staff.

'I know this is a difficult time for you. And I do sympathise with your current situation,' said one of the police officers in an attempt to calm Femi down.

'You can't sympathise with shit – it's not your sister that's been stabbed.'

'Look, Mr Adebayo, we're doing the best we can. We've seen an uptake in hate crime recently. And we're understaffed at the moment.'

'If this country has money to waste on nonsense like Brexit or supporting fools like Donald Trump, then you've got enough to go out and hire enough officers to make sure that justice is served.'

'Honestly, we're doing the best we can.'

'It isn't good enough!' snapped Femi.

'Do you even have any suspects?' asked Akinjade.

'The investigation is still ongoing.'

Thinking of previous incidents, Akinjade added, 'What about the Bronco brothers? They've been spreading racist propaganda for years and have attacked black people in the past.'

'They were cleared of those attacks.'

'Everyone knows they're guilty. It was a damn cover-up, and you know it.'

'You can't just go around accusing people, sir. You need proof. Look, we're following up every lead possible. We'll find out who was responsible for this attack. Until then, please let us do our jobs. If you can think of anything that may that may help us find out who it was that attacked your sister then please let us know immediately. But I think for now the best thing you can do is go and be with your family.'

Femi and Akinjade walked out of the police station in disgust at what they saw was a lack of urgency in finding out who was responsible for attacking Femi's sister.

'I'm telling you, Akinjade, any money if it was a white person who was stabbed the police would be out on the street interrogating and stopping any black person that they could find.'

'I feel you, Femi, I feel you.'

'This is the crap that makes me wonder why I bother with these people sometimes, Akinjade. I seriously want to go round to those Bronco brothers and knock them the fuck out.'

'As much as I'd love to see you do that, Femi, you'd get locked up. You've got a bright future ahead of you; don't waste it on those jerks. And you can't help your sister if you're in jail, can you?'

'Akinjade, since when did you become the voice of reason? Why don't we just go out and behave like Eric Killmonger and kill everyone who stands in our way?'

'Just letting off some steam, bro.' Femi and Akinjade exchanged smiles and had a little laugh between themselves.

'But the police were right about one thing, said Akinjade. 'There's nothing that we can do at the moment. Right now we're needed back at the hospital, Femi.'

'You're right – there's nothing we can do right now. Look, Akinjade, I'll meet you back at the hospital. There's something I need to do first.'

'You all right, Femi?'

'Yeah, there's just someone I need to see first. Thanks for taking time out to come down to the station with me.'

'Any time, Femi, I've asked one of my boys to open up the shop for me. I'll go into work later. Anyway, I'll see you back at the hospital.'

'I'll catch up with you later, Akinjade.'

As Akinjade headed back to the hospital, Femi went back down to Barking Road. He went back to the spot where he had first encountered the mysterious Mr Diggity.

'I really can't believe I'm doing this,' Femi thought to himself.

'Mr Diggity, Mr Diggity! Mr Diggity, are you here?'

'I had a feeling I'd see you again at some point,' Mr Diggity casually said as he walked towards Femi.

'Mr Diggity, they've hurt my sister. She's in hospital.'

'Calm down, Femi, easy there.'

'My sister's in hospital, fighting for her life. I can't be calm. I need to do something. The police are not doing anything, and I can't allow scum like that to go free. You're the only person I could think of that can help me do something about it.'

'All right, I hear you. The question is, Femi, what do you need from me?

'Your offer before; can you really go back in time?'

'Yes I can, Femi.'

'Is it really possible that we can make slavery disappear?'

'Yes, I have the means to make it happen.'

'If I do this, Mr Diggity, if I go on your mission to end slavery, will it save my sister?'

'I guarantee that if you do this what happened to your sister will *not* come to pass.'

'All right, I'm in.'

'Ok then, Femi. Follow me.'

Femi followed Mr Diggity down the side street.

'Where are we going?' Femi asked.

'You'll see.' Mr Diggity reached into his pocket and pulled out what looked like an electronic car key set. He tapped the Unlock button. Out of nowhere a door appeared. But this was not any ordinary door. It was glowing, and it shone with a royal ambiance. It was as if behind the door a divine power awaited them.

'After you, Femi.' Femi promptly walked up to door. Understandably, he was nervous; he had no idea what was behind the door. For all he knew he could have been about to be abducted by an alien. Deciding to take a leap of faith he opened the door and walked in. Mr Diggity followed him.

Femi was dumbstruck by what he saw. He was in a silvery glass room so shiny that the surface could act as a mirror. He was also able to see beyond the enclosure, which was surrounded by streams of continuous rainbow-themed rays. Within those rays Femi was able to see passages of time. He saw moments such as West Africa being invaded by the Portuguese in the 15th century; he saw Martin Luther King making his historic speech; he witnessed Man walking on the moon. In fact Femi was able to see all of human history from this place.

'Where *are* we?' Femi asked still in disbelief at what he was seeing.

'We're in what is known as the perennial realm. It's the barrier that sits between time. It's ageless, and this realm allows you to see all of time. That's why you're able to see every major event in history from this little enclosure.'

'Mr Diggity, this structure that we are currently in – what is it?'

'This enclosure, Femi, is called the Temporal Interference Management Electrical Mechanical Advanced Choice Hope Impossible Noble Evolver.'

'It's called a *what*?'

'Do I really need to spell it out for you? It's a Time Machine, you dummy! I swear you're meant to be a straight A student'

'Of course! each letter spells Time Machine. I can't believe I am actually standing in a time machine.'

'Told you I wasn't making this shit up.'

'So what are you; the Timekeeper?'

'More like an overseer; think of me as a guardian of time. I make sure that time flows as it should.'

'So you're telling me you're a black man's Dr Who?'

'Bitch, please, I'm for real. That fool gives time machines a bad name.'

'So what are you, then? I'm guessing you're not human.'

'I am what I am. Let's just say I was born to be the bearer of this mantle. But that's not important. What *is* important is the mission. Right, Femi, so let's figure out where you're going.'

'Going? But I only just got here!' Femi replied, a little puzzled.

'Slavery isn't going to end by itself. We need to figure out where and when to send you to make sure that this mission's a success. This will tell me.'

As Mr Diggity said this he pointed at a giant computer at the centre of the enclosure. He went over to it and began speaking to it softly.

Femi noted how there appeared to be some kind of binding between the massive computer and the rest of the enclosure.

'I'm guessing this computer's responsible for keeping all of this running.'

'That's correct. What I'm doing is plotting a course for you. I'm doing a check for all the major incidents related to slavery. This query will be finished shortly. Coming … almost there … bingo, here we are! Hmmm, that's interesting.'

'What did the computer find?'

'There have been 1,800 major incidents and time points in relation to slavery.'

'1,800!!! No wonder black people have been screwed,' Femi said, disgruntled.

'But that's not it. The interesting thing is these four points. Slavery seems to have stemmed from these four events. If we stop these events from taking place I believe that we will stop slavery from ever occurring.'

Femi, licking his lips and rubbing his hands in glee, asked, 'Ok, so where am I heading to?'

'Let's print a mission plan on the screen, shall we? Computer, please print out a mission plan for me based on these four events.' The screen phased into another mode and displayed a detailed breakdown of each part of the mission.

'Ok, here it is, Femi. Your first stop will be in West Africa in the 15th century. You're going back home, to the area now known as Nigeria.'

'Nice! It's been a while since I have been back there.'

'I thought you'd enjoy that. I'm sending you back to a year before the Portuguese are due to land there. You will need to find Chief Oko; you will recognise him as he's the one who wears this. It signified tribe leadership at the time.' Femi took note of the object Mr Diggity was pointing at.

'So, your first task is to find Chief Oko, learn his tribe's ways and help them stop the slave raids from being started by the Portuguese.'

'So you want me to find Chief Oko and do *what*, exactly? It's not like I can just tell him I'm from the future. I'm going to need to convince him to help me.'

'You have a point, Femi. Let's see what other information I have here on Chief Oko. According to the files he has three daughters, and a wife named Ayo. By the time you get there he'll have led the Yoruba tribe for ten years. He became leader of the tribe when his father died during the war with the Benin Empire. The file also says you need to be wary of Oba Esigie; he seems to have been the first man to have made contact with the Europeans. That should be enough to convince Chief Oko.'

'Understood. What's next?'

'Your second stop will be in 1831, at the time of Nat Turner.'

'I've heard about him. He led a famous rebellion, didn't he? He won many battles. History describes him as a great leader and warrior.'

'That's true,' said Mr Diggity. 'But they got him; he was captured and executed. Your job's to stop him from being executed and help him complete his rebellion, in order to free the land. This will prevent the civil war that follows. To do this you'll need to count on allies in places you wouldn't expect. When the time comes you'll know what I mean.

'Next, once you've saved Nat Turner, you're going to go aboard a ship, the Fredensborg, to be precise. It was used to carry slaves as cargo. You'll need to stop that ship reaching its destination, and rescue everyone on board. Are you following all of this?'

'Yes. So what's my last stop?'

'That'll be the Kush Kingdom. Find Queen Amanirenas; she led one of the few successful stances against the Roman Empire. Get her to ally with the Egyptians, and together they'll do more than make a stance. They'll beat the Romans and take down Caesar. This is the final part of the mission.'

'Why Rome? Why does my mission need to end there?'

Mr Diggity turned round and looked at Femi. With a sly smile he says to Femi 'That one you'll need to discover for yourself. If I told you now you wouldn't believe me.'

'Out of all the destinations, how come Haiti wasn't listed?'

'I'm guessing you're talking about the Haitian Slavery Revolt in 1804, Femi.'

'That's exactly what I was referring to, Mr Diggity.'

'It was successful, though, right?'

Femi nodded, 'Yes, it was successful.'

'That's exactly why you're *not* going there. We need you to go to places where slavery *wasn't* aborted. You're going to places where the impact will be widely felt. These places and periods in time are at the root of slavery. You're not going to address the symptoms, Femi. Your mission's to stop this disease from ever occurring in the western world in the first place.'

'All right, I'm on board with that. So how do I begin?'

'You'll begin with this, Femi.' Mr Diggity presented Femi with a bracelet with four beads in it. 'This device will allow you to time travel to each destination. Upon arriving in each one, its bead will disappear into a portal for safe keeping. The bead will also update your clothing to ensure you're wearing something appropriate for the time period in question. Each time when you've completed your mission, to retrieve it simply whisper *It's time to resume the mission*, and it'll reappear. When it does, one of its beads will glow like this one now, to highlight where you're going next.'

'Looks like I'd better get to work!'

'Before you go, Femi, I need to warn you. Should you succeed, the world you come back to will be no longer. Slavery will be gone and your sister won't have been harmed – but I can't guarantee that the world that you come back to will be as you expect. There are risks, and you will need to make sacrifices along the way. Also, you're going to have to do things that you never ever thought you could do. This mission's going to need a great deal of sacrifice and commitment. I'm not going to lie to you. This'll be the toughest thing you'll ever do in your life. If mission impossible was a reality, this'd be it. I ask you one final time; are you sure you're ready to do this?'

'This is the only chance I have, Mr Diggity. If I get this right it'll help so many people. This'll actually save the world. I *have* to do this!'

'Fair enough, very well then. We'll proceed when you're ready. Good luck. I'll check up on you when appropriate.'

'See you in the past, then, Mr Diggity.' Femi tapped the first glowing bead to begin the mission of a lifetime. A doorway opened. A storm surrounded the doorway. Femi walked into it and disappeared into the time stream, beginning his mission to end slavery.

Chapter 5: Chief Oko

Eventually the storm stopped and Femi found himself stranded on a beach. He slowly got up onto his feet and looked around.

'I guess this is it,' he said to himself. At that very second he saw his clothing had changed to reflect what people in West Africa wore during that time period, just as Mr Diggity had told him it would.

'Neat,' Femi muttered to himself. He started to wander around the beach.

As well as the heat he also noticed the natural beauty of the scenery. He thought to himself that perhaps he should stay there for a while and enjoy the surroundings.

'This is a side of Africa that the western media never reports on,' he remarked. He gave himself five minutes to enjoy the scenery and then proceeded to begin his mission. His first task was to find Chief Oko and locate the Yoruba tribe.

Femi walked for several miles along the beach, then he came across a river. He walked across it and continued on his journey. He continued walking for a couple of hours. Then he came across another river, with some children playing in the water. To avoid scaring them he decided to wait in the trees until he could see some adults so he could approach them to ask about Chief Oko. Eventually some women came to collect the children. Femi assumed that the women were the mothers so went over to them.

But as he went to approach them a man came from behind him and shouted, '*Iwo!*'

Femi turned around.

The man shouted again: '*Iwo!*'

Femi realised he was saying the Yoruba word for 'you'.

'*Tan e!*'

Femi, although not fluent in Yoruba, recognised those words too: 'Speak your name.'

'Femi Adebayo,' he responded.

He was surrounded by five more men. '*Kin o nfe?*' one of these men asked. Femi guessed that they were asking him what he wanted.

'Chief Oko. Take me to see Chief Oko.' These words startled the men.

'*Ni kiakia sile fun u* (hurry up and move)' one of them said. One of the men whacked him over the head with a stick. This knocked him out cold …

Femi woke up to find himself entangled in a net carried by several people. He looked around to try to figure out where he was. He noticed he was being carried into a village, with the people staring at him as if to say who is this? Who is this outsider being brought to us? They reached a hut located in the middle of the village, and dropped him just outside it, then one of his captors went inside.

After a few minutes he emerged with two men. One of them was an imposing figure who looked like he ate and wrestled bears for breakfast. The other was a classy gentleman who walked with poise and purpose. Femi took notice of the headgear that this man was wearing – he was wearing the item that Mr Diggity had told him to look for.

Femi said: 'Chief Oko!'

One of his captors hit him on the back and shouted at him, '*Si ipalolo.*'

Femi sensed that the best thing to do was to be silent. The captors went and started a discussion with the two men who had come out of the hut. This went on for a few minutes. Then Chief Oko walked up to Femi.

'*Si și i* (open it),' declared Chief Oko. The men then cut the net and helped Femi back onto his feet.

Staring at him point blank in the face, Chief Oko said to Femi '*Bawo ni iwo ti mo mi?* (How do you know who I am?)'

Femi responded 'I'm not completely sure what you just said – but Chief Oko, I need your help. I'm on a mission of great significance.'

'Hmm,' Chief Oko said in response. He grabbed a sword off one of his men. He pointed the sword at Femi and, this time shouting, he repeated: '*Bawo ni iwo ti mo mi?*'

Femi was really scared at this point, and didn't know what to do, so he started pleading: 'Chief

Oko, please, I'm no threat to you. *I* am not the danger. The real danger is coming. I'm here to help. Many people will die and suffer if you don't listen to me.'

Chief Oko put the sword down. He gave it back to his men. 'Ok, Femi Adebayo, what danger comes to us?'

Femi was stunned. 'You speak *English*!

'Languages have not necessarily come from where you have been led to believe,' responded Chief Oko. 'My name, as you seem to know, is Chief Oko. I'm the leader of the Yoruba tribe. I protect this land. So tell me who endangers us.'

'You may find it hard to believe what I tell you, Chief.'

'Try me, Femi.'

'I'm from a timeline in the future. In the time I'm from, black people have been made to suffer. They're treated like second-class citizens, have been forced from their homes and have never been compensated for this loss. They have been beaten, and raped, and forced to build other people's empires. I've been sent back in time to go on a mission to stop the events that have led to the enslavement of many people.'

'He he he. Ha ha ha ha ha ha ha ha ha ha. You have a wild imagination, my friend,' Chief Oko responded, amused. 'Where on earth did you come up with such a story?'

'I'm serious, Chief. You have to believe me. If you don't help me many people are going to suffer or worse.'

Chief Oko stood defiant. 'Ok, person from the future, prove it. Why should I believe you?'

'Ok then; you have three daughters, and a wife named Ayo. You've been leader of the Yoruba tribe for about ten years. You obtained leadership when your father died during the war with the Benin Empire. You know that Oba Esigie has been in contact with the Europeans, and you're fearful for the potential trouble that this may bring to your people. If I wasn't from the future, how would I know this?'

Chief Oko was stunned by Femi Adebayo's knowledge. He could see that Femi was telling the truth.

The man standing alongside Chief Oko said, 'Chief, kill this boy! He's a spy for Oba Esigie.'

'No, Femi speaks truthfully. Although I don't understand this future stuff that Femi speaks of, he knows things someone from our own time wouldn't know. All right, Femi, tell me what you know of the Portuguese.'

'A year from now they'll attack this place. Many people will be killed or taken away and enslaved. The westerners will then enslave people in many parts of Africa and institutionalise it around the western world.'

'If so,' said Chief Oko, 'my worst fears will have come true. But I've prayed to the spirits to help me find a solution to this problem, and *you* have come along. This can't be a coincidence. Men, release him. This Femi is not our enemy. He will help us.'

Chief Oko's men, as ordered, promptly untied Femi.

Chief Oko asked Femi, 'So, tell me, what do you know that can help us to stop the Portuguese from enslaving us?'

'I need you to let me fight alongside you,' Femi responds.

'Eh, fight alongside us? Boy, tell me how many fights have you been involved in?'

'I've had my fair share of fights in my time.'

'Really, Femi? Ok, tell me how many men have you killed?'

Femi fell silent. He knew he was going to have to fight, but the thought had never occurred to him that he would actually need to kill someone.

'Killed? I've never killed anyone, Chief Oko.'

'How do you expect to win a war, Femi, if you're not prepared to kill? Fights in the playground due to childish arguments are not the right preparation for going to war. Femi, if you're serious about taking on this threat, you're going to have to be prepared to do what's necessary. And that includes killing. You're going to need to take another man's life. Are you ready to do that?'

Femi walked up to Chief Oko and stared directly into his eyes. 'I'm willing to do whatever it takes to win this fight. I didn't come all this way to back down now.'

The men drew their swords and pointed them at Femi. Despite this, Femi did not back down, but continued to stare down Chief Oko. Chief Oko took note of Femi's stance and smiled.

'Very well, then. Guards, stand down. I see that you're eager to fight, Femi. But first let's do a little test. Let's have a little one-on-one fight. Try and land a punch on me.'

'You want me to hit you?' Femi asked, bemused.

'Yes, Femi, I do. Come on – you're not afraid of an old man, are you?'

Taking the bait, Femi aimed a swift punch at Chief Oko. He missed. He aimed another punch at Chief Oko and missed again. He kept trying and missing, until Chief Oko tripped him up and he landed on his backside. Chief Oko took one of the guard's swords and pointed it at Femi's face.

'You have courage and spirit, Femi, and are not afraid to stand up for your beliefs. These are very admirable qualities. But you're not a warrior. At least, not yet. You will stay with us and we'll train you. You'll become a Yoruba warrior. Your knowledge, I believe, will be essential in helping us defeat the Portuguese. Do we have a deal, Femi?'

'Deal,' Femi responded.

'Good.' Chief Oko extended a hand to Femi, which Femi accepted, and got back up on his feet.

'Guards, take Femi back to the village. Let him get cleaned up and get him some food. He has come from far and must surely be hungry.'

'Yes, Chief.'

The guards took Femi to the village as instructed.

The second man who came out of the hut with Chief Oko had witnessed what had just happened and was not impressed. He then went on to say to Chief Oko: 'Why do you entertain this, Chief? What can this fool boy offer us?'

'Have patience, my old friend. In time this boy will help lead us to further glory. He has a purpose. I do not think him showing up when he did was an accident; he is here by virtue. Also, if we don't help him he'll simply go out on his own and get himself killed. I cannot in good conscience let that happen. If we train him, he could help save our people. Make the preparations. He'll begin his training tomorrow.'

'Ok, Chief, but don't say I didn't warn you. I'd hate to have to say *I told you so.*'

Meanwhile the guards had escorted Femi to a hut in the middle of the village. They knocked on the door, and a young woman opened it.

'*Oloye Oko sọ pe o yẹ ki a mu u wa nibi* (the chief said we should bring him here)' one of the guards said to her.

'*Bẹẹni* (yes)' she replied. The guards left, and she grabbed Femi's right hand. '*Wa* (come)' she said, and Femi followed her.

Inside there were two other young women and an older woman waiting. Femi assumed she was their mother as he could see the family resemblance. They began to tend him to him. They offered him some water and food. It was the first bit of hospitality he had received since he had begun his mission.

After he had eaten he grabbed some buckets of water to wash himself outside the hut. 'This will have to do. Soap and toothpaste don't exist at this moment of time in this part of the world,' Femi said to himself, noticing the difference in how people of that time cared for themselves.

After Femi had finishing cleaning himself, he headed back inside.

'I see my family's treating you well, Femi.' He looked up and saw Chief Oko waiting for him.

'Your family … this is your family, Chief?'

'Yes, Femi. The three young ladies you see before you are my daughters. Allow me to introduce you to Adeola, Eniola and Iyin. And this is my beautiful wife, Ayo.'

'I'm honoured to meet you all. Thanks for your hospitality.'

'You'll be staying here whilst you train with us. We have a spare room you can use,' Chief Oko informed Femi.

'Sure, no problem.'

'You've travelled a long distance to get here, Femi. I can only imagine how hungry you must have been.'

'You have no idea, Chief! I was starving.'

'Well, my family will always make sure that you are fed, I assure you,' Chief Oko said with a small laugh. 'Anyway, we need to discuss why you're here. We need to talk about your mission. So you've come here to help us stop slavery?'

'Yes, I have,' Femi proudly responded.

Chief Oko smiled at Femi: 'I sense in you a kindred spirit, Femi. But you have a lot to learn. The mission you have undertaken is a monumental task. To complete it you're going to need to go through hell. We'll teach you our ways. If you're serious about succeeding, you must undergo the most rigorous training.'

Femi, keen to hear more, asked, 'What will you teach me?'

'We'll teach you how to fight like a Yoruba warrior. Here you'll study Dambe and Kokawa. We will teach you how to strike, Engolo, and Stick Fighting. We'll teach you how to move and how to think, and we'll make you mentally prepared for any danger that you may end up facing. I had prayed to the spirits for help as I believe a danger is coming to our lands. And here you are. I believe your arrival is the answer to my prayer. We'll need to make sure that no one is a match for you, physically or mentally. But now it's time for you to rest, Femi. You'll begin bright and early. Come, let me show you where you'll be sleeping.'

Chief Oko escorted Femi to the spare room and helped him settle into his new sleeping space. As the chief was about to leave, Femi said, 'Chief Oko, I have a question to ask.'

'Sure, go ahead.'

'This mission that I'm on. Be honest with me; do you think I'll succeed?'

'To be honest with you, right now you have no chance. You're not ready yet. You have the heart but you don't have the tools; at least not yet. But because of the danger that you'll face we'll have to make sure that we leave no stone untouched in your training. I believe in you, Femi. Be patient, endure, and you'll be ready when the time comes.'

'Thanks, Chief, I needed to hear that.'

'Anyway, good night Femi. I'll see you in the morning.' Chief Oko left the room and Femi went to sleep shortly afterwards.

Chapter 6: The way of a warrior

The next morning, Chief Oko woke up Femi at dawn and instructed him to get ready. After a few minutes Femi joined Chief Oko outside.

'So tell me Femi, what do you know about being a warrior?' asked Chief Oko.

Femi responded: 'How do you mean?'

'Simple, Femi, tell me what you think it means to be a warrior.'

Femi, pausing for a moment, stated, 'It's about taking out your opponent as quickly and efficiently as possible.'

Chief Oko looked at him and said, 'Ha! You have a lot to learn. Being a warrior is not a matter of being the fastest or the strongest. It isn't about how hard you can hit or kick or your opponent. It's more than that. It is about *why* you fight. It's about who you're fighting for. Anyone can attack, but not everyone can defend. Being a warrior is about being able to step up and be counted on when all the odds are against you. It's about fighting till the very end and fighting because it's the right thing to do. It's about having the will to do what is right, and fighting for those who can't fight for themselves. A

71

warrior fights with courage but also with honour. To succeed in the mission you're about to embark on, you'll face many challenges, and hurdles that you can't even begin to imagine. There will be times when you feel alone and have no one to help you. You'll have many hard tests and many challenging obstacles to overcome. But a true warrior will stand his ground and give it everything they have. Not because it's easy, not because of some self-righteous act, but because it's the right thing to do. Honour, courage and the ability to do what is right; this is the way of a true warrior. Remember this always. Understand?'

Femi gently nodded: 'I think so, Chief.'

'Good, now we'll begin. You have heart but no skill. You have the will but not the direction. Here we'll provide you with the skills to be become a true warrior. The skills we're about to teach you, you must master. Some day your life will depend on what you learn here. In fact I believe the outcome of your mission will depend on it.'

'Ade!' the chief then yelled. Ade, a giant of a man, approached Chief Oko and Femi, towering over them, and Chief Oko himself was no slouch. Ade stood with his hands on his hips looking Femi up and down to see what he was made of.

'You remember Ade, don't you Femi? He was with us yesterday. He will supervise your initial training. I'll see you soon, Femi. Ade, I'm leaving Femi in your capable hands.'

Ade walked around Femi but couldn't fathom what Chief Oko saw in him. Nevertheless, he decided to carry out Chief Oko's will.

'So you're the one who's going to save us from the Portuguese, hmm? Tell me something, boy, why should we train you?'

'Simple,' Femi responded. 'I'm here on a mission of greater purpose. I'm trying to save generations from now from going through a fate worse than death. My purpose in being here is to stop people from being taken into slavery. That, and your chief says your tribe will train me.'

'Ok, Femi, let's see what you've got.' Ade punched Femi in the stomach.

Femi fell to the ground and screaming in agony, said: 'What the hell was that for?'

'This is training Yoruba style,' Ade responded in a fit of laughter. 'You must be prepared for an attack from your enemy at all times. Get up and defend yourself.'

Ade lunged at him again, and while Femi ducked the first punch he was unable to dodge the second and third.

'Defend, Femi, defend. Fighting's not just about throwing punches and kicks. You have to be able to defend yourself and know how to avoid attacks.' Ade and Femi went a couple of more rounds but the pattern was always the same. Femi would avoid one or two punches then get caught by the third.

After taking a severe amount of punishment, Femi was struggling to get back to his feet.

'Had enough already? Is that all you've got? How do you expect to save people from slavery if you can't even protect yourself from me?'

At that point sudden anger flared within Femi. Ade's remarks had hit a nerve; Femi reminded himself of why he began this quest. He had done it not for himself but to help others. He wasn't taking this punishment for himself; he was doing it for the people and their generations to come. After a while he slowly got back to his feet.

'Stay down,' some of the tribe members were saying. Chief Oko was there watching. He could see Femi was in pain, but what he had seen in Femi when he had first met him was now on display for everyone to see. Femi had the heart of a warrior; he never gave in. This was a quality that would serve him well.

Femi knew that he had to try something else to avoid taking more punishment. He realised that Ade was stronger than he was, and so going toe to toe with Ade wasn't ever going to work. Instead he had to try to outmanoeuvre him.

'Come on!' Femi yelled. Ade lunged at him again but this time he missed. He threw another punch and missed again. He tried a couple more punches and in an instinctive move Femi rolled forward and kicked backwards to hit Ade from behind in the balls, then followed this up with a side leg sweep. The giant was down, to the amazement of everyone watching.

Ade angrily got up almost immediately. He saw Femi there, waiting to engage again as he had already resumed his fighting stance. Ade chuckled.

'Lucky shot! Maybe there is something that we can work with in you. You realised that you couldn't compete with me on strength and tried a different tactic. Not bad! It means, if nothing else, that there's a brain up there inside of you. Consider that as your first lesson: know your enemy, adapt, observe, understand how they fight, then attack. Get yourself cleaned up, then prepare for your next session, boy.'

Ade went off to prepare for the next round of training. Femi walked off, grimacing from some of the hits he had taken earlier on.

Members of the Yoruba clan approached him. Emeka said to Femi, 'You're either very brave or very stupid. However, I think Ade's starting to like you. I've seen him do far worse to others for so much as even glancing at him wrongly.'

'You call that liking someone? That Ade's a nutter. He was trying to knock me out cold. I can only imagine what he has planned for me next.'

'He's training you, Femi. Trust me; at the end of all of this you'll see why Ade was so hard on you.'

For the next few months Femi went through torture. Ade took Femi to the breaking point. Ade piled it on Femi during training, never allowing him a breather even for a moment. Femi was beginning to wonder whether he'd been a fool to think that he could accomplish what seemed like an impossible mission. He was struggling to master the techniques that he was being introduced to. He was well aware, too, that time was not on his side and he had to get his act together fast.

After one such long day Femi returned to his hut. Exhausted, he just lay there on his bed. He began to believe he'd made a big mistake: 'What on earth was I thinking? I'm in way over my head.'

'What's this? You're giving up already? I told you this wasn't going to be easy.' From the shadows a mysterious figure emerged: Mr Diggity.

'Oh, it's you.'

'Nice to see you too, Femi.'

'What do you want? I mean, what are you doing here?' Femi snapped.

'I'm here to check up on you, Femi. Thought I should see how you're holding up. How are you enjoying 15th-century West Africa?'

'Are you taking the piss? I'm hungry, I've been battered, battered some more and run into the ground. I am not ok at all.'

Mr Diggity smiled. 'Good.'

Femi, confused, struggled to his feet: 'Good? How is this good?' he asked.

'Because now you're starting to get a glimpse of how people in slavery felt,' Mr Diggity said sharply.

'I thought my mission was to *end* slavery.'

'It is, Femi. But it's like that old saying. How can you provide a solution when you don't even know what the problem is?'

Femi began to calm down and sat down on his bed. 'You're not going to make this easy for me, are you?'

'If it was easy I wouldn't need to send you back in time with a time machine. If it was easy, someone else would've found a way to stop slavery a long time ago. It could be worse. Trust me; compared to what others have suffered you're getting off lightly. Just remember you're here by choice. There are others who've not been so lucky.' Mr Diggity walked up to Femi and sat down beside him.

'Look, Mr Diggity, I know in some kind of psychotic, weird way you're trying to prepare me for what's to come. The real question I have is why am I here? I mean why do I need to start here? I mean, why is it I'm not fighting the Roman Empire or changing the fate of Nat Turner? What's my purpose here?'

'You really don't know why you had to come here first, Femi?'

'No, Mr Diggity, I don't.'

'All right, let's try to see if you can answer your own question. Tell me … let's say that I sent you to the Kush Kingdom to get their queen on your side right now, this instant. What would you say?'

Femi shrugging his shoulders said, 'I don't know.'

'Ok, then let's say you're up against the Roman Empire, and by that I don't just mean Caesar's soldiers. I mean his gladiators. Warriors of legend like Flamma. What chance right now would you stand against any of them? I'm serious. Tell me!'

'I'd find a way to win.'

'Find a way to win? Huh! Femi, you're either reckless or a damn fool. Look at how you've fared any time you've faced Ade. The Roman gladiators would eat you alive! Even for the rescue of Nat Turner, do you have a plan? Do you have a strategy in place for accomplishing that? Do you even know where you'd begin to look for help? This is the mission to end slavery, not a suicide job. The reason you're here in West Africa is, to put it bluntly, you're not ready for what lies ahead for you after this. The reason you're here is to learn how to be a fighter. You need to know what it means to suffer, and you need to know what it means to win at all costs. You need to know how to look deep into your soul and go to places where you've never been before. You need to develop the ability to look death in the face and piss on it like it's nothing. If I sent you to those places now, you'd fail. But once you're a warrior, someone who is capable of leading an army, someone who has the skill and the will to overcome any adversary that you face, then and only then will you prevail.'

Femi was disheartened by what Mr Diggity said. He slumped deeper into his bed sheets. But deep down he knew Mr Diggity was right. Femi just didn't want to give Mr Diggity the satisfaction of seeing that Femi knew he was right.

'Heh, chin up,' said Mr Diggity. 'It's not all that bad. You're still standing. You're still here. You've only just started your journey. You haven't even reached half time yet. Let me tell you a little story. You know Batman, right?'

'Batman?' Femi bewildered. 'What does *Batman* have to do with this?'

'Yes, Batman. The Dark Knight Detective himself; the scourge of criminals in Gotham City,' responded Mr Diggity. 'You remember how he began, right? He witnessed the death of his parents at a young age; he was driven by vengeance. But he didn't go out there and start taking on criminals straight away. He went away from Gotham to learn the skills that he'd need to fight for justice. He had to acquire the tools that he'd need to become Batman. And at the end of the process he became something truly special. He became a legend. If you look at everyday real life, think about all the successful people you know of. I mean success stories like Denzel Washington, Michael Johnson the athlete, Barack Obama or, closer to your home city, John Boyega. They didn't start off as famous or successful as they are. Most people only look at the finished article, and forget the journeys that these successful men all took to get where they are now. If you want to be something special you have to put in the work. And this quest that you're on is no different, Femi.

'You know something, Femi? I could have sent anyone on this mission. There are billions of people living on this planet in the time you're from. Yet out of all those billions I chose you. A black kid from east London whose anger and hardships stopped him from seeing what was in front of him. You have the ability to be something; greatness is inside you, kid. Yes, you're here because you care about your people. Yes, you're here because deep down I know you want to make a difference. But most of all, go out there and do it for *you*. So cut out this nonsense. Take your beatings; take your medicine, as it were. And learn from your mistakes. This is the environment for you to master what they're trying to teach you. At some point in the future everything you've learnt here, and will learn, will not only save your life but will be the key to you succeeding. Now go out there and prove me right.'

Now, from being disheartened, Femi felt happy. 'Wow, you know something, Mr Diggity? That was the best pep talk I've ever received. Thank you; I think I needed that.'

'Good. Now get some rest, you're going to need it tomorrow. Right now it's time for me to get going. I'll check on you later.' Mr Diggity stood up and reached into his pocket to grab his time machine key switch. With a tap on a button a door opened; he disappeared into it and within a whisper was gone.

Just after Mr Diggity had vanished, one of the chief's daughters walked into Femi's room: 'Are you all right Femi? I thought I saw a light.'

Smiling Femi responded, 'Thank you, I *am* all right. In fact I feel great. I can't wait till training begins tomorrow. I'm going to destroy whatever they throw at me tomorrow. Good night.'

Femi was left alone to sleep. As he lay down on his bed, one thought went round and round in his mind: 'I'm ready. Let's do this.'

The next day a transformation had taken place in Femi. Mr Diggity's words had really hit home. Instead of thinking about the pain he was in, he turned all of his focus onto the mission. Little by little he started to make progress. He started to win duels with other members of the tribe. As Femi's confidence grew he started being able to beat even the best Yoruba warriors. Ade and Chief Oko looked on and saw Femi's transformation firsthand watched.

'Femi's made good progress, Ade.'

'Eh well, he doesn't suck as much as he used to. Oh all right, the kid's proven that he has some character.'

'Character, Ade? He's shown more than that. He's even beating some of our best fighters, Ade. For someone who a few months ago didn't know how to throw a punch properly I'd say that's impressive. I think it's time to take him to the next stage of his training.'

'Wait, Chief – do you want to prepare him for the tests? Normally it takes at least three years before we consider putting anyone forward.'

'Normally I'd agree. But he's the key to stopping the Portuguese. Plus he has shown he can learn quickly. I'll take him with me to oversee his final phase of training, to begin his preparation for the tests.'

'Very well, Chief. I wish you good luck.'

Chapter 7: Why do you fight?

During the four and a half months since Femi had first come to West Africa to begin his training, he found that he had been pushed to the very limit both physically and emotionally. He had endured so much. But he understood that this was necessary, to prepare him for the dangers and challenges ahead of him. The success of the mission depended on it.

One morning he woke up to find Chief Oko already in his room waiting for him to awaken.

'*E kaaro*, Femi,' said Chief Oko.

'*E kaaro*, Chief,' Femi said, understanding that the chief had said good morning to him.

'*Se o sun dada* (Did you sleep well)?'

'*Beni* (Yes, of course), Chief.'

Chief Oko then asked, '*Setan fun ọjọ miiran ti ikẹkọ* (Ready for another day of training)?'

Femi said, '*I wa setan lati ja* (I'm ready to fight).'

'Excellent! You've picked up some of our language during your time here, Femi. Very good indeed. Since you're ready to fight, get changed. A special part of your training begins today, Femi.'

'Sure, no problem.'

'I'll wait for you outside, Femi.'

Femi wondered to himself what could be so special about today's training. Nevertheless he got ready, then left the hut to meet up with Chief Oko.

'I'm over here, Femi,' Chief Oko shouted.

Femi ran over to join him. Chief Oko had several items on the ground: two sets of spears, two sets of Nguni shields, some wood and an interestingly shaped sword with a strap.

'Femi, I want you to grab one of each of the items that you see on the ground and follow me.'

Femi picked up one of each item.

'You're beginning to look the part now. Are you set?'

Femi, nodding his head, replies, '*Beni.*'

'Good. Ok then, Femi. Now follow me.' Ade was also there, waiting for them. Chief Oko called him over.

'Ade, me and Femi will be travelling east to begin the final part of his training. Until I return you're in charge of all matters with the Yoruba tribe.'

'Yes, Chief,' responded Ade.

'Come, Femi, we have a long journey ahead of us, and there is still much to be done.'

Chief Oko and Femi then began their journey. They walked for a couple of hours. Along the way Femi was taking in the sights and enjoying the scenery. They went back along the beach that he had walked along when he had first arrived in 15th-century West Africa. The journey reaffirmed what Femi had always known; Africa at its best was a land of beauty, harmony and paradise. The beaches that people of the 21st century often go to see in places like Miami can also be found in Africa. The major issue is how Africa is so often portrayed in the media.

Noting how Femi was paying keen attention to the environment, Chief Oko said, 'Beautiful isn't it?'

A smiling Femi replied, 'Yes, it is.'

'Femi, that might be the first time I've ever seen you smile. You have a beautiful smile, Femi – you need to use it more.'

Femi laughed at Chief Oko's comment, but replied, 'The world hasn't given me a lot to smile about in recent times.'

'Really? Please do enlighten me.'

'Maybe later, Chief Oko, but right now I'd like to enjoy the view as we continue our journey.'

'As you wish, Femi, as you wish.'

Then they reached a river.

'We have reached our destination. This is the Niger River. It is the biggest known river in our land. This is where you will begin your next phase of training. But first we need to eat.'

'Eat? But Chief, we didn't bring any food – we only brought weapons.'

Chief Oko started giggling.

'You find my response amusing, Chief?'

'Animals in the wild don't wake up with food to eat. They go out and get their food. They go hunting for their prey. Femi, you need to know how to survive. To survive you must know how to hunt.'

'All right, then, so where do we start?'

'Firstly, Femi, who said anything about *we*? And secondly, where do you think?'

Femi looked around and then realised that Chief Oko meant the river. 'Of course, you want me to go fishing.'

'Exactly! Now get busy; I'm starving.'

Femi went to the river.

'Stay on the edge Femi, and be careful not to go too deep. There can be predators about.'

'Oh, so now you tell me.'

Following Chief Oko's instructions Femi stayed close to the edge of the river. He waited patiently. After a while he started to see fish appearing. Immediately he lashed out at them with his spear but the fish escaped. Another few fish came by, and again he lashed out at them and again the fish escaped.

'Patience and subtlety are what are needed, Femi. If your enemy can see your attack they'll be able to avoid you. Don't rush. Time your attacks, but most importantly let the enemy come towards you.'

Heeding Chief Oko's words, Femi decided upon a different tactic. When the next few fish arrived instead of immediately lashing out at them he stood there silent and still as a shadow. Instead of swimming away from him the fish swam towards him. Eventually the fish were within a whisper of him. In a sudden flash he jammed his spear into the river. When he retrieved it he saw that a fish was stuck onto it.

'Very good, Femi, now do it again.'

He repeated that approach, and the next time he caught two fish. He began to hit his groove and was beginning to catch fish like there was no tomorrow. In the end he managed to spear twenty fish.

'Excellent work, Femi! Now we can eat. You see these pieces of wood? We'll use them to make a fire for our feast.'

Chief Oko then took a couple of pieces of wood, rubbed them together and made a fire. They then sat down to enjoy their food.

'You know something, Chief Oko? That's the first time I've ever been fishing. In the end I really enjoyed it.'

'When you understand how to do something then the enjoyment will come. This fish is tasty. It's a good meal. You've earned this feast.'

After finishing their meal Chief Oko and Femi sat down and just enjoyed the wonderful view of the Niger River.

'So, Femi, tell me; you mentioned earlier that the world hasn't given you much to smile about. Why's that?'

'It's a long story, Chief.'

'We'll be here for a while, Femi. We have time.'

'Where I come from, black people don't have it easy. We have to fight twice as hard, we have to prepare twice as hard and we have to study twice as hard just to sometimes stay afloat. I live in a system designed to keep black people down. I come from a world where when people think of Africa they don't think of beautiful scenery like this. All they think of is poverty, corruption and disease. I come from a period where for many generations black people have been treated like second-class citizens. At times I've had to fight obstacle after obstacle after obstacle, and it is still doesn't feel enough. It's like a never-ending battle without any reward.'

'Sounds like you've had to deal with a lot, Femi. Tell me, does your father know about how you feel? Perhaps you can talk to him, to help.'

'I lost my father when I was four. He died of cancer.'

'Cancer? What's cancer?'

'It's a deadly decease that kills many people every day. If you can diagnose it on time there is a chance of survival, but we were too late.'

'I'm very sorry to hear that, Femi. No child should have to grow up without a father. Do you have any brothers?'

'No, but I have two sisters; one older and one younger.'

'So you've had to carry the family mantle. That explains a lot.'

'Care to elaborate, Chief?' Femi asked intently.

'Certainly; when you first came to us you had a lot of anger. You were eager to head straight into battle. Yet you didn't have the skill or the wisdom of how to succeed in battle. But the will was there. You've grown tremendously in your time with us.

You've taken on every challenge that we've thrown at you, and every time you've fallen over you've got right back up and come back at us twice as hard. Soon you'll be ready to truly go on your quest.'

'Thank you for your kind words. You said that I will soon be ready. So the question I have is what's missing? What else do I have to do?'

Chief Oko put a hand on Femi's right shoulder. 'As much as you've learnt, there are still things that we need to teach you, especially in terms of how to engage opponents in a one-on-one situation. You also need to pass a test to join us officially as a Yoruba warrior.'

'A test?' Femi replied.

'Yes; a test. When the time comes we'll discuss this some more. I'll make sure you're ready. Your fighting ability is not what concerns me, especially when I look at what you've learned already. The thing that worries is this: tell me, Femi, why do you fight?'

Femi stared at Chief Oko and said, 'I don't have a choice. I *have* to.'

'Really? So you're telling me that no one else could have gone on this quest? What made you come here?'

'Simply because I had no other choice. I couldn't sit around and not do anything. My youngest sister was badly wounded when I started this quest. I'm doing this to avenge her. But also I'm doing this for my family and my people. No one should have to suffer what black people have suffered in my timeline.'

'Ok. Your reasons for fighting are pure and genuine. There are some men that just fight for themselves and don't think about anyone else. They are selfish, and they're just fighting for their own glory and their ego. But you're fighting for a higher purpose. That will give you power and resolve in your darkest moments. If you learn nothing else from your time with us, just remember that. Remember why you're really here. Remember what you came to achieve on this mission. That will drive you on to gain victories and gain wins when you're on the verge of defeat. Trust your instincts and let your heart guide you when you're on the battlefield. Does it make sense what I am telling you, Femi?'

'Yes it does, Chief.'

'Ok then; now, are you ready to resume your training, Femi.'

'I was born ready, Chief.'

'All right; it's time for me to teach you how to be a swordsman. On your feet, Femi. Grab your sword and stand ten feet in front of me.'

Femi, as instructed, got to his feet and went to grab his sword.

'The sword you have is called the *Ida*. It's laced with pepper and poison to make even the smallest cut deadly to your adversary. The sword, however, is not the weapon. The person who wields it is the weapon. You must be as one with the sword. You must view the sword as an extension of yourself.

Treat the sword as you do your own life. You must value the sword the way you value your own life. Now, we're going to start with some basics. Follow what I do. This is the guard stance.'

Femi took his sword and, following Chief Oko, got into the guard stance.

'Good; maintain a firm grip on the sword, but not so hard that you lose your sense of motion. If your grip's loose not only will you lose the sword but also your life. Keep your feet shoulder width apart, with one foot slightly forward. Now let's begin with some basic defensive manoeuvres. We'll start slow. Head!'

Femi got into the head stance.

'Good. Now left shoulder. Steady, right shoulder. Pause. Now left leg. That's good; keep your balance at all times. Now let's speed it up slightly. Head, left shoulder, right shoulder, left leg. That's very good. Now do it again. Head, left shoulder, right shoulder, left leg. Head, left shoulder, right shoulder, left leg. Head, left shoulder, right shoulder, left leg. Head, left shoulder, right shoulder, left leg – and back flip, but maintain a grip on your sword.'

Chief Oko did a back flip. Femi, confused, followed suit a few seconds later. 'Why did you add a back flip into the routine?' he asked.

'It may at times be necessary, as sometimes in a fight you may find yourself on the back foot. A simple move like a back flip or even a shift to the left or right can give you the distance you need to get yourself back into the fight and disturb your opponent's rhythm. Understand?'

'I think so, Chief Oko.

'Excellent. Now let's do some attacking stances.'

'The same positions that you use to defend yourself you can also use to attack. However, you have another move you can do. It's called the thrust. As before, Femi, repeat everything I do. Head, right shoulder, left leg, thrust. Head, right shoulder, left leg, thrust. Head, right shoulder, left leg, thrust. Head, right shoulder, left leg, thrust – duck!' Femi ducked at the end of the sequence.

'Nice! Head, left, shoulder, right leg, duck, thrust, head. Nice! Now do it faster. Head, left, shoulder, right leg, duck, thrust, head, roll forward, thrust. Left shoulder, right shoulder, head, back flip. You must always keep your opponent guessing. Vary your attacks. Again, even faster; left leg, thrust, thrust right, thrust left, left leg, right shoulder, now *attack!*'

Chief Oko then leapt at Femi and Femi instinctively blocked with the head stance.

Scared, he shouted, 'What are you doing? Are you for real?'

'This is part of your training, Femi. To be a swordsman you need to know how to engage your opponent. Now fight. Defend. Use your eyes, look at where the sword's going.' Then Chief Oko attacked Femi from all sorts of different angles – head, right, left. Femi was ducking and diving, weaving and waving, defending for dear life.

'What's the matter, Femi? Are you afraid to take a swing at me?'

Femi angrily took a wild swing at Chief Oko – who simply ducked out of the way and then tripped Femi over. As Femi was about to get up Chief Oko placed his sword one inch over Femi's head. Femi, sensing Chief Oko standing above him, had no choice but to hold his position. He knew at this point he was at Chief Oko's mercy.

'A second later your head would have been off. Never allow yourself to lose control. In a fight you must always stay in control. Fight with courage and honour. But don't be foolish. Do *not* make rash decisions. Anger may prepare you for the battle, but it's a lousy weapon. Also your opponent may say things to put you off your game. Don't be influenced by that. Let this be your first lesson. Does it make sense what I'm saying to you, Femi?'

Femi gave a gentle nod to acknowledge where he had gone wrong.

Chief Oko withdrew his sword and offered Femi his right hand: 'Come.'

Femi gladly accepted, and Chief Oko helped him get back on his feet.

'Well for someone who's never held a sword before you didn't do too badly. So don't be too hard on yourself. This is what training's for. If we fall, we get back up. If we fail, we keep trying until we eventually succeed. In this environment we can learn. I'd rather you learned here than when you face what you'll have to face down the road in your journey.'

Femi smiled: 'Thank you Chief Oko. I don't think I could have asked for a better teacher.'

'And I feel I couldn't have asked for a better student. It's my honour to help you with your quest. So, shall we continue?'

Femi, smiling, drew his sword, got into the guard stance and said, 'Ready when you are!'

Chief Oko reciprocated the gesture and said, 'All right. One, two, three ... *attack!*'

For many months Chief Oko and Femi practised swordplay. During this period Femi gained an understanding of footwork, grappling and how to anticipate the moves of his opponent by studying his eyes. Femi was beginning to become a complete warrior. Chief Oko saw Femi's skills advancing at first hand. They had many test duels; on many occasions Femi would come close to beating Chief Oko, but Chief Oko's experience always enabled him to come out on top. Nevertheless, Chief Oko knew that soon Femi would be ready to truly begin his mission.

But before Chief Oko could conclude Femi's training there was one thing left for Femi to do. He had to beat Chief Oko in a one-on-one sword fight.

'Femi, we've been here many months. In this time your skills have become exceptional. You have the speed, the movement and the coordination. In terms of pure fighting skill there's nothing you're lacking. I've taught you all that I know. Now it's just a matter of fine-tuning your instincts. Now it's about acting and reacting before your opponent can even blink. Master this and you'll be invincible. You have honoured me, Femi.'

'Thank you, Chief Oko. It's been my pleasure to learn from you.'

'Today marks the end of your official training in sword duelling. The next thing for you is to face the tests of a Yoruba warrior. But first you must beat me. To win you need to get me in a killing position or I must yield. Now, prepare yourself.'

At the moment Chief Oko took out his sword and got into his battle stance, Femi did the same.

A silence grew. You could only hear the whisper of the grass and the River Niger. The stage was set for a final pupil vs master duel. It was samurai against samurai. It was gunslinger against gunslinger. It was time for Femi to earn his stripes, and graduate and take the next step in fulfilling his mission.

'ATTACK!' yelled Chief Oko.

Their swords came together in a thunderous clash. Then strike after strike, you could hear each impact of the swords for miles. From thrust to head, shoulders, knees and toes, it was an even match. This was not a case of Femi duelling with his superior. Now he was battling Chief Oko as an equal. After several minutes of duelling, the two warriors' swords were stuck; neither man could force an advantage. In a change of tactics, Chief Oko struck his left arm round Femi's face. Femi promptly did the same thing to stop Chief Oko from gaining an advantage. The two men back flipped into their head stances to give themselves breathing space and a chance to regroup.

'Good, you knew to hit me back to stop me from pressing home the advantage. I've trained you well.'

'I've had a good teacher,' Femi responded.

Because Femi and Chief Oko had been training together for months they knew each other. They knew each other's footwork and manoeuvres. They knew what tactics they often would employ, and they knew each other's weaknesses. For a winner to emerge it was going to take one of them to do something different and unexpected.

They re-engaged, and traded strike for strike. Chief Oko ducked a head swing and Femi jumped a low attack. Their swords came together once more. Chief Oko managed to make Femi drop his sword. It was advantage Chief Oko. Chief Oko took swipes at Femi but Femi wouldn't yield. He avoided one of Chief Oko's attacks by rolling forward. Spotting his sword he did several back flips to recover it, with Chief Oko in hot pursuit. At the very last second Femi was able to regain his sword and block Chief Oko with a back head stance. With their swords locked in position Femi slowly got back to his feet. Femi knew that now he had Chief Oko where he wanted him and if he was going to win this duel, now was his window of opportunity.

Using all the willpower he had left he rammed Chief Oko in the stomach with his left elbow. He spun round and did a roundhouse kick to leave Chief Oko off balance. Then he kicked Chief Oko's sword out of his hand. Chief Oko fell to his knees in shock. As Chief Oko's sword dropped, Femi grabbed it. He then held both swords over Chief Oko's head, crossing each other. as if he was about to behead Chief Oko.

'Yield,' said Femi.

The battle was over. Femi had won. The pupil had finally beaten the master. Both men were breathing heavily. Chief Oko looked up at Femi with a frown across his face. Within a matter of seconds that frown had turned into a smile. Chief Oko applauded him.

'Brilliant! That was absolutely brilliant. I knew there was a warrior inside you. I knew that with you we have something special. You have shown heart, courage, wit and quick thinking. Even when you dropped your sword you didn't give in. You fought on just like you've been doing ever since you came here. Now you're the master of the sword. And I couldn't be prouder!'

Femi withdrew the swords. 'Are you ok? I'm sorry if I hurt you.'

'No need to apologise, Femi. When you train people, as well as dishing out the hitting you have to be prepared to be hit as well. It's all part of the job.'

'But I could have killed you.'

'Yes, Femi, you could have but you didn't. And that was because you're now in control. You knew you had the battle won. Discipline is also required to be a great warrior.'

Femi offered his hand. Chief Oko gladly accepted and got back on his feet.

'So what do we do now, Chief?'

'It's time we went back to the village. We've done what we came here to do. But first let's recover. Rest and eat we must. That, and give me some time to help me get over this defeat. At least going forward you'll be fighting by my side.'

At that moment both men laughed out loud. Chief Oko and Femi had developed an unbreakable bond. Chief Oko had never had a son. Femi had grown up for most of his life without a father. In each other they were able to provide something they had both felt was missing from each other's lives. It was this bond that made their relationship special.

Femi and Chief Oko spent the next few hours resting and eating, and nursing their bruises from their final duel.

Chief Oko entertained Femi with stories from his youth. Especially the time he first encountered an elephant: 'I'm telling you, it was huge. I had never ever seen anything that big. I just stood there in wonder. I was fascinated by how the spirits could create a creature so big.'

'Weren't you scared?' Femi asked.

'No, I actually wanted to ride the elephant.'

'What stopped you?'

'My father! He found me and said, 'Son, ah ah, come over here now, jor. Aya now. That elephant's not a toy. Get here now.' Both men laughed at the story.

'You know something, Chief? I've really enjoyed my time here. I've loved training with you. I've enjoyed getting to know this part of Africa. I'll be sad when I have to leave.'

'We've loved having you here as well. However, if you don't want to leave, then why not stay?'

Femi was stunned by Chief Oko's suggestion. 'Stay? I can't stay here.'

'Why not? Why can't you stay? I mean, what's stopping you? You've become one of us. You're part of our tribe now. As far as we're concerned you're family.'

'It's not that simple, Chief. Look, I feel blessed that you want me around. But it isn't that simple. I came here on a quest. I came here on a mission. I made a commitment, and I need to see it through. If I don't, then a lot of people in generations to come are going to suffer. Make no mistake, the Portuguese will soon be here. I need to be ready. We have to be ready. When we've dealt with the Portuguese I'll need to move on. There are other people in the world that'll need my help going forward.'

Chief Oko was a bit disheartened by Femi's response. But deep down he knew Femi was right.

'I hope my response hasn't offended you, Chief.'

'No, Femi. You haven't offended me at all. It's just that I have three daughters waiting for me back in the village. They're beautiful children and I'm blessed and privileged to have them in my life. But meeting you has been like gaining a son. You've given me a happiness that only comes when a man passes on his teaching to his son.' A tear rolled down Chief Oko's face.

'Ahh, Chief, please don't cry,' Femi said, then went to sit beside him. 'You've given me something too. You've shown me what it's like to have a father. It is something I've missed out on. I feel exactly the same way.'

Femi and Chief Oko hugged each other as if they were father and son.

'Anyway I'm not going yet. Our work isn't done here. You also need to finish telling me about the tests, Chief.'

'Tests?'

'Yes, the tests. The ones you said I need to complete to become a Yoruba warrior.'

'Ah yes, of course. Sit down, Femi, and I will tell you all about them.'

Femi sat down.

'Your training's complete. Physically and mentally you have everything you need. But to become a Yoruba warrior you have to face what we call *Igbeyewo Gbẹhin*; the ultimate test. You'll have to pass three tests. The first is a test of will. It's about using your willpower to overcome what seems like an impossible task. Not unlike your mission. The second is a test of strategy. Being a warrior isn't just about your fighting skills. You also need to have a sharp mind. On your journey you'll face armies greater than your own, warriors whose strengths dwarf your own. Or you may find yourself stuck in a tight corner. In those moments it's about finding a different solution; you've got to be smart and out-think your opponent. This test is about proving your ability to be smart on the battlefield. If you get through those two tests and if you have enough strength and endurance left, a final challenge will await you. Your final test will be a test of might. When you pass the tests, then and only then will you officially become one of us. Only when you pass these three tests will you become a Yoruba warrior.'

Femi paused for a moment. He then let out a broad smile and began laughing.

Chief Oko was quite annoyed at Femi's response. The chief needed Femi to take these tests as seriously as his training. 'What's so funny, Femi? This isn't a joke. I'm serious.'

'I know. I mean *only* three tests. Is that it? You make me do all this training and then all I have to do is pass three easy tests? This has to be a joke.'

'These tests are sacred to our people. Show some respect.' Chief Oko stood up, stared down Femi, and continued angrily, 'I didn't put all this effort into training you for you to fail now.'

Femi realised that he had angered Chief Oko. In fact in all the time Femi had known Chief Oko he had never seen him get so angry. Femi knew he had messed up big time here.

'Chief, I apologise. I didn't mean to offend you, your people and your customs. That was never my intention. Please forgive me.'

Chief Oko calmed down: 'Apology accepted. Femi.'

'It just feels like with everything I've taken on since I've come here, the way you describe those tests makes them seem very underwhelming.'

'I assure you Femi, they're a lot more difficult than you realise.'

'Even so, surely I've demonstrated all the skills those tests are asking of me anyway?'

'Indeed you have Femi, indeed you have. Nevertheless our custom cannot be ignored. These tests were designed to act as a confirmation that you've not only undergone the training but that the message has sunk in. They're your final examination. As you said earlier, your time with us will soon be at an end. When you move on from here to continue with your quest I'll no longer be around to help you. You'll be on your own. Hopefully along the way you'll meet others who will happily join your noble cause. But make no mistake. Femi; you have a long and dangerous journey ahead of you. These tests will also give you the best possible preparation to face those challenges head on. Trust me, your mission will have a better chance of success once you've passed these tests. If anything, I guarantee that what you endure on these tests will at some point save your life.'

'All right, Chief, you've convinced me. I'll take these tests. Not only will I take these tests – I'll smash them. I'll crush them and pass with flying colours!'

'That's more like it, Femi. There's the fine warrior I have been training these past few months.'

'So, Chief, when do these tests begin?'

'We'll begin them tomorrow. Your first test will take place not too far from here. The last two will be back in the village. Now we must rest. You'll need all your energy for the first test. Get some sleep.'

'All right, Chief, tomorrow I'll begin the tests. Good night.'

'Good night, Femi. Sleep well, young warrior, sleep well indeed.'

Chapter 8: Man vs beast

Chief Oko confirmed that Femi was coming face to face with his first real danger.

'Good to know, Chief,' said Femi. 'But how in the hell are we going to survive this?'

Chief Oko sensed the fear creeping into Femi. He could hear his own heart beating faster and faster: 'Calm yourself, Femi. Focus and show no fear. Lions are predators. Predators will jump on you if they sense you're afraid. Just remember your training.'

Getting a grip on his emotions, Femi stared at the lions in the hope of spotting something that would give him and his chief a chance of survival. His eyes were fixated on the lions as it dawned upon him the scale of the danger that they suddenly found themselves in. He softly drew his sword. He was ready to strike.

'Patience, Femi. Watch their movement. They outnumber us. Wait for them to make the first move then attack. Watch their feet.'

Femi, acknowledging Chief Oko's advice, observed that one of the lions took a slight step backwards. Seeing this, Femi knew that the other lion was going to attack first. And so it proved. As the lion jumped at him, Femi stabbed the lion. Wounded, the lion fell to the ground. It let out a roar; it was in pain and its roar was a roar of agony. Sensing an opening, Femi stabbed the lion again. It fell silent and died.

The second lion charged at Femi, no doubt enraged by what Femi had done to his fellow pack member. Before, the lion had been just hungry, but now it was out for blood. Femi managed to block the lion's initial attacks with his shield. That was enough to keep it at bay for the moment. But the lion was relentless; with his life hanging in the balance Femi knew if he made one wrong move it would be enough to get himself killed. He noted that there was a tree behind him. Remembering the acrobatic defensive moves he had learned during his training, as the lion came at him again Femi threw mud in its eyes, this was enough to temporarily block the lion's vision, giving Femi the time he needed; he ran towards the tree. The lion followed in pursuit.

With the adrenaline rush of desperation running through his body, as Femi approached the tree he ran right up it and using his momentum with all the force he could muster he did a 360 degree flip off the tree, confusing the lion. As Femi began his descent, he managed to strike the lion in the back. Landing on top of the lion, he stabbed it again, finishing the job.

Femi had managed to slay two of the lions. Taking a moment to gather himself, and when the adrenaline rush slackened, Femi remembered there was a third lion.

'Chief!' Femi said, worried. He rushed back to save his chief.

Whilst Femi was facing off two of the lion pack Chief Oko had engaged the third. The lion was on top of Chief Oko, whose shield was the only thing saving him from certain death.

'*Chief!*' shouted Femi as he threw one of the spears towards Chief Oko. Chief Oko grabbed the spear and stabbed the lion, ending the threat.

Femi ran to Chief Oko and helped him get back on his feet. 'Are you ok?'

'I am, Femi, I lost my footing and the lion leapt on top of me. You saved me today, Femi. Thank you.'

'You saved me first. It was you training me that allowed me to prevail.'

'We should move on, Femi. This area is no longer safe. There may be other lions.'

'Agreed, Chief.'

Femi and Chief Oko grabbed their belongings and headed off towards the place where Femi would be taking his first test.

'I can't believe we just fought off a pack of lions. They're amongst the most dangerous animals,' said an exhausted Femi.

'You did well today, Femi. You have proven your courage, will and ingenuity again tonight.

There's nothing else for me to teach you in terms of fighting. I have no doubt you'll pass the tests.'

'Thank you, Chief. But this is just the beginning. There are still more dangers that I'll have to face. What scares me is I don't know what they'll be.'

'Life will always throw up dangers and challenges. We can't be prepared for everything. But I know you'll be ready regardless of what danger comes your way,' Chief Oko said firmly. The two warriors continued their journey. They eventually stumbled upon a cave which would keep them safe till dawn. They settled in and got some rest.

Chapter 9: The first test – a test of will

At the crack of dawn Femi and Chief Oko began their journey. They headed south. It was here that Femi would meet his first test. Around midday they reached their destination.

'Where are we, Chief Oko?' Femi asked.

'This mountain's called Chappal Waddi. It's our highest mountain – well, the highest one we've discovered, anyhow. Your first test is a test of will. You must climb this mountain. At the top you'll find a rare type of purple flower. Pick one of them. This will prove that you've reached the top. This is the test.'

'I understand, Chief.'

As Femi got his things and get ready to set off on his first test, Chief Oko Femi placed a hand on his right shoulder: 'Femi, before you depart there is one more thing I need to tell you. Once you have acquired the flower don't head back down the mountain immediately. Before you return, I want you to take a moment to observe your surroundings. When you are on top of the mountain, practise your swordplay and the fighting techniques you've learned in your time with us.'

Femi was a little puzzled: 'Chief, if this isn't part of the test, why would you request this of me?'

'When you get back to me you'll understand. Do this, and you'll have found something that'll make you not just a greater warrior but a better man.'

'All right, Chief, I trust you. I'll do this for you.'

'Thank you, Femi. I'll be waiting for you here when you return. Now it's time for you to begin your first test. Good luck.'

Femi began his climb. Chappal Waddi was a high mountain, and although Femi had weapons he had no food and water. At times during the climb he was in pain. But regardless of how much pain he was in, he was determined to reach the top. He knew that those aches and pains were all part of the test, and that this was a vital part of him becoming a Yoruba warrior.

A few hours later, Femi had reached the top of the mountain. He looked around, saw the purple flowers, and picked one of them. He was about to head back, but then he recalled Chief Oko's final set of instructions to him. He placed most of his gear on the ground.

He looked around at his surroundings. The view from the top of Chappal Waddi was beautiful. He felt in harmony and at one with himself. It was almost as if he could clearly hear his thoughts.

'I could stay here and observe this view for eternity,' Femi said to himself. He drew his sword and began to practise the manoeuvres and stances that he had spent months mastering. This time around, though, Femi felt a difference. He felt smoother, slicker, faster. He felt more instinctive in his fighting style. Previously he had felt that he had to tell himself what to do with his sword, constantly reminding himself of all the lessons he had learned during his training; but now he knew what to do and when, without even having to think about it. He had gone to another level.

Femi practised for an hour. He wanted to continue even longer, as he felt he was in an environment where he could be at peace and one with himself. But then he thought about his mission and why he was really here. He thought about what had brought him to 15th-century West Africa in the first place. He knew it was almost a year since he had first set foot in West Africa, and that the threat of the Portuguese was looming. Femi knew he would have to face them head on, otherwise his mission would have failed before it had truly begun.

He gathered his equipment and prepared to head back down the mountain. But then he took one final glance at the view he had from Chappal Waddi. And he heard a familiar voice.

'You've grown stronger since I last saw you. Physically and mentally you've become something else. Now you're one arse-kicking machine. I wouldn't want to face you in a one-on-one battle.'

Femi turned round. 'Mr Diggity, trust you to go and ruin a perfect view.'

'Femi,' blushed Mr Diggity. 'Is that any way to greet an old friend?'

'Old friend! More like the man who's sent me on a quest of doom.'

'I gave you the option to go on this quest. I didn't force you into it. You accepted.'

'Touché, Mr Diggity, touché.'

'Well, it did take something major to happen to your baby sister for you to accept my offer.'

'Don't go there, Mr Diggity. Remember I'm the one carrying the sword laced with poison, and I know how to use it.'

'Heh, I'm on your side. Sorry, I shouldn't have gone there. Sensitive subject I know. I was just trying to break the tension. Call it my twisted sense of humour.'

'I accept your apology.'

'Mind if I join you and enjoy the view? After all it isn't often you sit on top of a mountain like this.'

Femi nodded, and Mr Diggity promptly joined him.

'It *is* a nice view,' Mr Diggity remarked. 'I can see why you don't want to leave this place.'

'I know.'

'I wasn't talking about the mountain, Femi. I was referring to this place in general, West Africa.'

'I'm not sure I understand what you mean.'

'I think you do, Femi, I think you do. I mean, look at this place. It's peaceful, you have beautiful people. You're with a group of people that have taken you on as one of their own without any question or hesitation. That hasn't always been the case in your life. You're thriving on the challenge that's been presented to you. In Chief Oko you have even found a surrogate father. These are things that anyone would love to have.'

'It's true, Mr Diggity. I do feel happy here. I'm happier than I've been in a very long time. But I know I can't stay here. I need to finish my mission. If I don't, many people will suffer and all of this will have been for nothing.'

'Well Femi at least you haven't let your heart rule your head. That's a sign of maturity. My advice to you is to enjoy your time here. You've earned it, and I'm pleased you're happy. There's no point going on an impossible quest if you can't enjoy the adventure as you go along, right?'

Femi, smiling, nodded back in agreement with Mr Diggity, and said, 'Right.'

'I have just one last thing to tell you, Femi. Please be very careful of attachment. Attachment has seen many good men go off track. I mean, just look at Anakin Skywalker in Star Wars.'

Femi and Mr Diggity burst into tears of laughter.

'You're trying to teach me a life lesson and you use Star Wars. I like Star Wars, but *really ...*' laughed Femi.

'What's this? Have you become Master Yoda or something? You don't know the power of the dark side of the force, young Femi,' Mr Diggity responded, still laughing. 'I love Star Wars. You can't go wrong with a Star Wars film. But on a serious note, Femi, just make sure you keep your head in the game. Remember your training, and remember the real reason why you're here. Understand?'

'Understood, Mr Diggity,' Femi responded.

'Good. Well, as always it was good catching up with you. Remember when you're done here whisper the command *It's time to resume the mission*. Your time bracelet will reappear and it'll highlight where you need to go next. Tap the bead that's glowing and you'll be transported to your next destination. Until then, and see you later Femi.'

Mr Diggity reached into his pocket and pulled out his time switch. With one tap on a button the time door appeared.

Before Mr Diggity disappeared back into the future Femi asked: 'Mr Diggity, just one thing that I noticed. Why is it you can just drop in on me any time you please but I don't have any way of calling upon you? What if I get trapped or need you?'

Mr Diggity with a big smirk, said: 'Simple – it's about keeping you on your toes. Also, if you could call me any time you wanted this mission would fail. If you had access to a get out of jail free card all the time, you'd never figure out how to stop going to jail in the first place. Think of it as the whole *teach people to fish and they'll feed themselves* philosophy.'

'Hmmm, point taken,' said Femi. Mr Diggity waved Femi goodbye then walked back through the time door.

Femi took some time to think about what Mr Diggity had just told him. He wondered if he would have developed the fighting skills or the knowledge that he now had if he could have just called upon Mr Diggity any time he wanted. He also began to wonder if his mission was deeper than what Mr Diggity had told him so far.

'Too many questions to answer now. I'll address them another time.' He took one last look at the view from the top of Chappal Waddi.

Then he suddenly felt hungry: 'Hmm, I haven't eaten since this morning. I hope Chief Oko has got stuff for us to eat.' Femi gathered his belongings and started the long trek back down the mountain.

A couple of hours later Femi found himself back at the bottom of the mountain. As promised, Chief Oko was waiting for him. Chief Oko had started a fire and had some food ready for him.

'Ah, Femi, welcome back; I was starting to wonder whether you'd got lost. Here was me thinking I'd have to finish all of this by myself.'

Femi walked up to Chief Oko. He dropped his equipment. He gave him the purple flower.

'This is excellent, Femi, very good indeed. You've completed the first test.'

'Thank you, Chief Oko.'

'So Femi, when you reached the top of the mountain how did you feel?'

'Great!' responded Femi.

'Did you train up there as I asked you to?'

'I did indeed. When I was up there, for some reason I felt transformed. It's hard to explain but I felt at peace. I felt harmony in body and mind. I felt

I had balance. I felt my sword was doing the work instead of me. Why was this?'

'It's because you've found something, Femi. You were in touch with your warrior spirit.'

'My warrior spirit, Chief?'

'Yes, Femi, your warrior spirit. You achieved equilibrium. You were in control of your emotions. You had liberated yourself. Those surroundings gave you a platform to be liberated. You were in a place where there was no fear, no doubt, no limit. When you get to that point there's nothing that is beyond you. That is why I wanted you to practise whilst you were up there. Although that's not the only thing that you found whilst you were up there, was it, Femi?'

'I don't recall finding anything else whilst I was up there Chief?'

'Is that so, Femi? Tell me how did you feel whilst you were climbing up the mountain?' Pausing for a moment, Femi cast his mind back to what he was thinking and going through whilst he was travelling up the mountain.

'At times I was hungry, tired, hurting and in pain. At times, if I'm honest, it was pure torture.'

'But despite all those odds, Femi, you still prevailed. Why was that?' Chief Oko asked.

'Simple. It was because of the mission. I wasn't prepared to fail now. The Portuguese are coming soon, and I have to be ready. Anything less than victory is not good enough. If I fail now, then the mission's going to be over before I've even started.

I guess I wasn't prepared to accept defeat. Giving up was never an option. I guess all I had was my body, my guts and my will. There's a saying where I come from: *While there's life there's hope.*'

Chief Oko smiled at Femi's response. 'Now you understand. You understand that there's a fine line between success and failure. You know what it takes to win, because you understand what it takes to lose. If you give up, even for a moment, that's all it takes to lose the battle. In life, as you know, you're going to go through hardship. Nothing comes easy in life, let alone the quest you're embarking on. Sometimes when you're staring defeat in the face you have to dig deep and really go to the limit. Climbing that mountain, you pushed yourself to the limit again, just like you have throughout your time here. You've gained resolve. Regardless of what happens when the Portuguese come, remember everything you've overcome since you've been here with us. When you're at your deepest and darkest moments, think back to what you did here, and you'll never go wrong. The greatest weapon you'll ever have isn't a spear; it isn't a sword or a shield. It's *you*. You are the wielder of a weapon. You control how the weapon functions. Your will and resolve will allow you to overcome any opponent or obstacle that you face. Never ever forget this.'

'Thanks, Chief.'

'Now, Femi, I don't know about you, but I'm starving. Come, let's eat.'

Femi gladly sat by the fire and started tucking into the food that Chief Oko had prepared.

'This is really good, Chief! What is it?'

'Goat.'

'I love it!'

'We'll rest here tonight, then we'll head off in the morning. We'll go to where your final two tests will be.'

'And where are we going tomorrow, Chief?'

'Don't tell me you've forgotten, Femi. We're going home, Femi, back to the village. We've been away for a while now. I'm starting to get a little homesick. I need to get back to my daughters. That, and I'm the leader of the Yoruba tribe. My people need me.'

'I agree,' said Femi. 'It'll be good to see everyone again.'

'Even Ade?' said Chief Oko.

'Well, most people.'

Femi and Chief Oko shared a laugh, and continued on with their meal. After they had finished eating Femi reflected on Chief Oko's comment on Ade. It was as if he sensed that Femi didn't like Ade.

'How did you know that I had a problem with Ade, Chief?'

'I sensed the tension between you two when we were leaving the village,' Chief Oko replied.

'Honestly, Chief, I don't know what I did to offend him. Forgive me if I say something horrible,

118

but I feel he's just had it in for me from the moment he met me.'

'I understand why you feel that way, Femi, but don't be so quick to judge him. We're all unique in our own way. Everyone has their own means of communicating and instructing people. He has helped protect my people on so many occasions, and would gladly lay down his life so that others can live.'

Femi was intrigued by Chief Oko's admission. He wanted to know more: 'It sounds like you and Ade go way back.'

'We do, Femi.'

'Care to shed some more light on this?'

'Hmm, it appears that you want another bedtime story, Femi. Very well then; I hope you're sitting comfortably.

'I've known Ade since we were kids. We grew up together. We played together and when it was our time to become Yoruba warriors we trained together. The first time we met, however – now, that was a story. Ade was at the river collecting water for his family. I was out and about playing in some nearby trees. Out of nowhere I heard this roar. I hid in the trees. A few moments later I saw this huge silverback gorilla. I had never seen a gorilla before and I was fascinated by it. So I decided to follow it, keeping in the shadows of the trees. Then it reached the river where Ade was; he turned round and saw it, and the gorilla roared at him and approached him menacingly. Ade was cornered and it looked as if the gorilla was going to get him.'

'You and Ade faced a gorilla?' Femi gasped. 'How the hell did you survive?'

'To be honest with you, I have no idea. I think the spirits were watching over us. To this day I still don't know what possessed me to do this – I looked around and noticed there was a fishing net lying on the ground. I snuck out of my hiding place, grabbed the net and managed to throw it over the gorilla. I shouted at Ade *'Come quickly!'* Me and Ade ran as fast as we could. Eventually the gorilla got free from the net and came after us in hot pursuit. We got back into the shadow of trees and found one to climb up. Then we waited quietly until the gorilla got there. It looked around and eventually moved on. When we were certain that the gorilla had gone, we climbed down and got away. Ade thanked me for saving his life. I told him, *'No problem'*. We exchanged our first names and that was the beginning of a lifelong friendship.'

Femi was impressed by this: 'Wow! A friendship forged by avoiding a gorilla. Is it me, or do you have a penchant for attracting attacks from wild animals?'

'I don't know. Perhaps they like my smell.'

Femi and Chief Oko shared another laugh.

'Since then, Ade's been by my side. He's a valiant warrior. But more importantly he has a good heart. He may be tough on you, Femi, but he understands the mission you've undertaken. He only wants you to be ready.'

'Being tough is not what bothers me, Chief. I felt he didn't like me from the get go. It's like I did something to him.'

'It is not you he doesn't like, Femi. It's who you remind him of.'

Femi was confused by that: 'Remind him of? Do I resemble someone he knew?'

'No Femi; it isn't a matter of resemblance. Ade used to have a son. He loved that boy dearly. He wasn't that much older than you are now. Many years ago Ade and me fought in a civil war. This is when the Yoruba tribe was first being formed. We had neighbouring tribes who opposed our inception. Me and Ade were put in charge of protecting the village from the oncoming battle. Ade told his son not to fight as he hadn't completed his training. They argued for many days about this, and then wouldn't even speak to each other for a while.

'The day of the battle came. We suffered heavy losses and the battle was going quite badly until a young warrior entered the fray and helped turn the tide. He had remarkable speed and skill. He was cunning, too. When we'd won the battle the young warrior approached me and Ade, removed his mask and revealed himself. He was Ade's son. He had disobeyed his father. But what should have been a triumphant coming of age moment turned into disaster. One of the enemy, who had been badly wounded and had appeared dead, managed to throw a spear into his back, killing him instantly. His bravery had saved our village, but at a terrible cost. Ade never forgave himself. He had to bear something that no father should ever have to bear; burying his own child. Ade swore to never again let a young man go into battle until he was fully prepared. This is why he has pushed you as hard as he has.'

Femi was stunned at what Chief Oko had told him. 'This all makes sense. I get it now. He doesn't want what happened to his son to happen to me or anybody else. All this time I had been answering him back, and I was thinking that he had no faith in me – whereas in reality it was actually the complete opposite. Thank you, Chief, for clarifying this.'

'You're welcome, Femi. So when we return back to the village, cut him slack. Despite his tough exterior he has a good heart. He has the best of intentions for you. Does that make sense, Femi?'

'Yes, Chief. I'll view him with different eyes now. Sometimes, unless you understand the context you can never really know a person.'

'Exactly, Femi, exactly. Now get some rest; the journey back to the village awaits us tomorrow.'

'All right. Goodnight, Chief. I'll see you in the morning.'

Chapter 10: The second test – a test of strategy

After months of being away from the village, Chief Oko and Femi finally made their way back there. As one of the villagers saw them, he shouted 'Our Chief has returned! Our Chief has returned!' Everyone in the village stopped what they were doing and ran to greet them.

Chief Oko and Femi were surrounded. The reception they received was akin to that of a war hero returning home after the call of duty.

'My thanks to you all. It's good to see you're well. Where's Ade? I must speak with him at once.'

'Yes, Chief.' One of the villagers went off to find him.

Chief Oko was greeted by his family – his daughters, Adeola, Eniola and Iyin, as well as his wife, Ayo. Chief Oko kissed his wife and hugged his daughters.

'It's good to see you, my love,' said Ayo.

'It's good to see you too, Ayo. I've missed the warmth of your hands and the joy your presence brings me.'

'And how is our young warrior doing?'

'Femi is doing superbly. He's mastered the art of sword fighting and has passed the first test. I am confident that he'll soon become a Yoruba warrior and fight alongside us.'

'I've missed you, Dad,' Adeola said, in joy at her father's return.

'I've missed you too.'

A few moments later an imposing voice was heard. A voice that was only too familiar to Femi.

'Welcome back, Chief.' Ade had been found, and bowed to greet the chief.

'Rise, my old friend; we have much to discuss. Femi, please go back home with my family. Get some food and some rest. Today you take a breather, and then tomorrow you'll face the second test.'

'Yes, Chief Oko. Femi headed back to the hut with Chief Oko's family.

'So, Chief,' said Ade. 'Femi managed to pass the first test; I have to admit I am surprised. How was his sword fighting?'

'It was exceptional, Ade; he managed to beat me.'

'Femi actually managed to beat you, *really*?'

'Yes. There's something special about him. Now he has the fighting skill to match the sprit he showed when he first turned up here.'

Ade couldn't believe what he was hearing. But he was beginning to revise his opinion of Femi: 'Who knew that little boy could make such a fine warrior?

So, for the second test what will you have him do, Chief?'

'I have an idea. To undertake his mission, he will need to think outside the box to defeat his enemies. I want this test to prepare him to do that. Inform Golibe; tell him to prepare himself for tomorrow.'

'Golibe? You don't mean you want Femi to face Golibe? Nobody's beaten him in five years. But Femi has never played that game before. Don't you think that'll be putting him at an unfair disadvantage?'

'Will he have any advantages when he is facing down the Portuguese in the near future, or any other adversary that he'll come up against? You of all people must understand this.'

'As you wish, Chief Oko. I'll inform Golibe immediately.'

'Before you go, Ade, how have things been in the village? More specifically, has there been any news from Oba Esigie?'

'Everything's been fine, Chief. He's been quiet. No one has heard from him in years.'

'That's what worries me, Ade. Based on what Femi's told me, Esigie will be the one who brings the Portuguese here. We must stay alert. If you hear of anything please bring it to my attention immediately.'

'Of course, Chief.'

At midday the next day Chief Oko escorted Femi to the centre of the village, where his next challenge awaited him. Before Femi was a table, and a man sitting down on the other side of it. The table had on it an ancient board consisting of twelve pits. Each pit had four stones in it.

'Welcome to your second test, Femi. Today is a test of strategy. To pass this test you'll have to use your mind. This is Golibe, the resident champion of a game called Nayo. He hasn't been beaten for five years.'

Femi, perplexed, turned round to face Chief Oko. 'Hold on a second – you want me to beat this guy who hasn't lost at this game for *years*? What kind of nonsense is this? I've never played this game in my entire life. This isn't fair!'

'Do you think the Portuguese will give you a head start when you face them? Well then. You faced down lions but you get scared of a little board game?'

Despite his irritation, Femi sat down to face Golibe, asking Chief Oko: 'So, what are the rules?'

'Allow me to explain, Femi. The aim of the game is to capture more stones than your opponent does. Each player takes turns to select a pit and spread the seeds in that pit around the board. When one of the pits has five or more stones you may capture them. When there's one pit remaining, the person whose side of the board it is will claim those stones. The first player to win five games will be declared the winner. Understood?'

'Understood, Chief.'

'Very good; now begin. Good luck. May the best man win. Golibe, as the defending champion, you can go first.'

Golibe picked the second pit to move the first set of stones.

'Your turn, Femi.'

After taking a few minutes to analyse the board he chose to move the stones from the fifth hole.

'Interesting choice.'

The first game went on for about ten minutes. When the game ended, Golibe ended up outscoring Femi by 3 to 1: 'First round to me. You still have the option to quit if you want.'

'Let's go again, Golibe. You still need four more games to win.'

'All right then, Femi, I'll even let you go first.'

The second game also went on for about ten minutes. Femi again found himself on the losing side. He would need to change tactics quickly or he would be on his way to a straight whitewash. He began to think back to the lessons he had learned whilst he was training under Ade and Chief Oko. He realised that Golibe had the edge on him in terms of experience and knowhow. Golibe had been playing this game for many years. Femi would have to find a way to throw Golibe off his game. He had to find a way to get inside of Golibe's head. In short, he would need to play mind games on him.

'What's the matter, champ? Scared that you're going to lose to an amateur?' Femi said in a bid to break Golibe's concentration.

'Excuse me?'

'You heard me, champ – stop taking so long. Hurry up and move.'

In a hurry Golibe moved some stones. 'I've moved; your turn.' Golibe had fallen for it. His move allowed Femi to capture the last two set of stones in the third game. This move allowed Femi to win the round and get on the score board. This irritated Golibe, and he threw his hands up in frustration.

'Temper, temper, champion!' Femi commented, hoping to rattle Golibe even further.

'*Ole* (thief), reset the board. You won't win this. I'm the champ. No one can beat me!'

Sensing his opportunity, Femi was able to rattle off two more rounds to pull ahead. As the game went on, they started to draw a crowd. No one had even seen Golibe taken this far before. They were intrigued in how this match was going to turn out. Everyone in the village was curious to see who was going to emerge the victor.

Then Golibe managed to even the scores. It was four games each. Femi had started the game as an amateur. But now he was battling Golibe as an equal who was only one game away from claiming victory. The next round would determine the winner. As the last game went on, the tension could be seen in both Femi and Golibe. Sweat was pouring down Golibe's face; having started the game confident, he was now panicking and doubting himself. Femi, too, was a nervous wreck –

he needed to win in order to move on to the final test, to complete his training. Meanwhile, Golibe was trying to defend his title and his reputation. That last game went on for almost hour. Each man took their time contemplating their next move; one wrong move could swing the round in either man's favour.

After an hour's play all that remained was one final stone on Golibe's side of the board. Picking it up, Golibe smiled, believing that it would be enough for him to seize victory. Chief Oko came in to count the stones. Golibe and Femi anxiously awaited the outcome of the count.

To Femi's relief and the crowd's surprise Femi had beaten Golibe by a single stone. Femi had passed the second test, albeit by just one stone. Golibe was not happy. As well as being a bad winner he was a sore loser. He smashed up the board and left, humbled; for not only had he been beaten, but he had lost to an outsider who had never played the game before.

'Well done, Femi. You continue to amaze me,' Chief Oko said.

'Thank you, Chief.'

'Tell me, how did you beat him, Femi? Ade asked in astonishment. 'Many have tried to beat him for years, and nobody's ever got anywhere close. We could barely win a single round off him.'

'I had to beat him up there,' Femi responded, pointing to his head. 'I can't touch him in terms of move set or experience, as he's been playing this game for many years. But if I could get inside his head, if I could make him lose his confidence and his focus, then I knew he would be vulnerable. No one's unbeatable; the trick is to make yourself as hard to beat as possible.'

'You've spoken like a true Yoruba warrior,' said an impressed Chief Oko.

'Not yet, he isn't. There's still one final test remaining,' Ade reminded Femi and Chief Oko.

'Then let's proceed to the final test, tomorrow, Ade,' said Femi. 'It's time to finish this. I'm ready.'

Chapter 11: The final test – a test of might

The day of Femi's final test had finally arrived. Femi had overcome every challenge that the Yoruba tribe had presented him with. There was only one test remaining – the test of might – before Femi could be granted the status of a Yoruba warrior.

Before Femi began his final challenge Chief Oko addressed him in front of the other warriors.

'Femi Adebayo! You've done well in your time with us. You've grown as a person as well as a warrior. You've even saved my life! For that I'll be forever in your gratitude. Nevertheless, in line with our traditions, before we can anoint you officially as a Yoruba warrior there is one final test that you have to pass. Your final challenge awaits you. You've shown that you have the willpower; you've proven that you can think like a warrior. Now you have to prove your might. Today you face the gauntlet.'

'What do I need to do to in the gauntlet?' Femi asked.

'Simple, Femi. All you need to do is to acquire that emblem over there.' As Femi looked ahead he saw a miniature wooden statue of a Yoruba tribe member wielding the *Ida*.

'Is it that it? All I need to do is grab that statue?'

'Yes, all you have to do is grab that statue. That statue is a symbol that recognises you as a Yoruba warrior. Claim it, and you've passed all of the tests.'

'All right, Chief, no problem.'

'Not so fast, Femi – *Awọn jagunjagun jade* (Warriors, come forth)!'

With those words four warriors entered the scene and lined themselves up, equally spaced from each other. The warriors were all that stood between Femi and his prize.

Femi, now fully aware of the task in front of him, responded: 'Chief Oko, now I get it; to get the statue I need to go through the four of them.'

'What? You didn't think it would be that easy, did you? Standing before you are four of the best fighters that our tribe has to offer. Each of them is responsible for protecting their section. Once you get past one you go on to face the next, and so on and so on. Get through all four of them of them and only then will you become a true Yoruba warrior.'

'Very well then; all right, let's do this.'

'Collect your weapon from Ade,' Chief Oko said. Femi warily walked up to Ade to collect it. Expecting another rude and unsavoury remark, he was surprised at what Ade said to him.

'Good luck, Femi. I'll see you at the end, warrior.'

Throughout all his training Ade had seen first hand how Femi had had to sweat blood and tears to get this far. During that time Femi had earned Ade's respect. Now Ade wanted him to finish the job. Femi took an ironwood sword and shield, and set about facing the gauntlet.

Femi approached the first warrior and got into his battle stance.

The chief shouted, 'Femi, are you ready?'

Femi gave him a nod as he stared down his first opponent.

'Warriors, are you ready?' The four warriors gave a chest fist-bump to signal their readiness.

'Then begin.'

Femi's final challenge was under way. The first warrior had a Bo staff and used its length to make jabs that kept Femi far away from the statue. At first he made thrusts to keep Femi at a distance. Every time Femi tried to advance he would run into the Bo staff. After a few minutes Femi and the first warrior were at a stalemate. Then Femi, taking a second to reflect, thought about what the target was for this exercise. His target was to get the wooden emblem; it wasn't to necessarily beat the four warriors in front of him. Deciding to change his tactics he came forward again. This time, though, when the Bo staff was in reach he was able to trap it on the ground with his sword, and he took the opportunity to trip the warrior up and leap over him, to advance to the second warrior.

'Round 1 complete!' shouted Chief Oko.

The second warrior charged at Femi with a wooden club. He was very strong, and swung wildly at Femi, who continually had to duck and dive and use his shield to block the attacks. The second warrior was relentless and unleashed a barrage of wild swings at Femi. Eventually he let out a monstrous growl and managed to knock Femi's shield out of his hand. Femi back flipped away from the warrior, confusing him, then darted forward and made tried to get his shield back, but the warrior came at him, repeatedly kicking his shield away. In a daring move Femi kicked the warrior in his manhood, making him collapse.

Femi got back on his feet and ran to meet the third warrior. Deciding to go straight into the attack, Femi leaped into the air and unleashed a double bicycle kick that instantly took out the third warrior; the speed of Femi's attack had left the third warrior with too little time to react to what he was seeing.

Then there was only one. In an almost mirror match, Femi was confronted with a warrior using the same weapons that he had: a sword and shield. But now Femi found himself starting to tire, and barely had any energy left to mount a defence. He was drained by the three combats he'd just won, and then he suffered a strike to his chest that had him gasping for air.

Unexpectedly, an unlikely source yelled out, offering some words of encouragement.

'Is that it? Is that all you've got?' Ade yelled. 'After all you've been through, are you really going to quit now, huh? You took down two lions, for crying out loud. Remember your mission; *the Portuguese are coming!'*

With those words Femi was able to get his second wind and drag himself back onto his feet. Looking deep within himself he willed himself to continue: 'C'mon, let's finish this.'

The final warrior again went to engage Femi, and both men unleashed everything that they had at each other. After a series of strikes, Femi managed to disengage his opponent and took him down with a roundhouse kick.

With all four warriors defeated, Femi reached out to claim his prize. He grabbed the statue and held it aloft for everyone to see. Femi had achieved his first milestone. He was at last a Yoruba warrior!

Ade applauded and Chief Oko quickly followed. Everyone joined in the applause. Appreciating the effort Femi had put in, the four warriors saluted him. The outsider had become one of them, and was now ready to aid them in the upcoming fight against the Portuguese.

Chapter 12: Stopping the Portuguese

Femi had successfully passed the tests. The next day he knelt before Chief Oko, to be officially accepted into the tribe as a warrior.

'Femi, when you came to us you were a boy with a heart of gold but you had no direction. You lacked the tools to do what was necessary. Through your courage, willpower and skill you've earned your place amongst us. Now rise, Yoruba warrior.'

Femi rose to his feet.

'I'm honoured, Chief. But our task isn't over yet. I've been here almost for a year, and the Portuguese will be arriving soon. We need a battle plan.'

'You're right, Femi. My concern right now is that we don't know much about the Portuguese. We don't know what weapons they have; we have no idea how big their army is. We don't even know where they'll strike. We need this information.'

All of sudden gunshots were heard, and screams.

'What's going on?' Ade asked.

'This can only mean one thing, Ade,' said Femi. 'It's the Portuguese. No one in this country has weapons that make that sort of noise. They're here!'

Chief Oko said, 'Ade, get the rest of the men and tell them that the time to fight is *now*. Femi, Dele, you two are with me. We'll hold off the invaders until the rest of the men get here. Get your weapons.'

Femi, Dele and Chief Oko hurried to confront the enemy. A group of eight Portuguese soldiers had entered the village and started to ransack the place. The screams got louder, and blood started to be spilled as the soldiers laid waste to the village.

In a fit of rage Femi threw his spear at one of the soldiers. The spear landed in his skull, killing him

The commander of the soldiers, seeing this, said in a rage, 'Nigga, I'm going to rip out your heart for this.' He swivelled his arquebus towards them, and told his men to aim likewise.

Femi, Dele and Chief Oko dived for shelter behind the stone wall that surrounded their village. The gunfire took chunks out of the wall.

Femi knew that they could not go into a full-scale assault, as the Yoruba armour was not designed to withstand gunfire. However, he spotted one weakness with the Portuguese weaponry. He noticed that after every shot there was quite a delay for reloading.

'Dele, Chief, stay here until they stop firing. When each of the soldiers have shot their guns, they have to reload. That takes time, so that's the moment we attack. We go in fast and hard. Kill first, ask questions later.'

Chief Oko agreed with Femi: 'Ok, Femi, on your mark we'll tear them to shreds. We'll go on your order.'

Another volley of gunfire came. Grabbing their spears Oko, Dele and Femi waited for the reload interval.

As the gunfire stopped Femi shouted, 'NOW!' Running out and launching their spears, they killed two more soldiers. This caused panic in the Portuguese. Femi got close enough to slit the throat of another of them whilst Dele pierced the heart of another. Femi went on to disarm one of the other soldiers and beat him into submission.

'You bastard! You'll pay for what you've done,' Femi yelled at the soldier as he unleashed blow after blow on him until the soldier stopped breathing.

Chief Oko had killed two of the remaining soldiers but was keeping the last one alive. Dele and Femi rushed to join the chief.

'Why are you letting him live?' Dele asks.

'We need information. He'll give it to us. Then he'll pay for the harm he's done to our village.' The chief pushed his sword right up against the soldier's neck.

'How many are there of you? Where are the rest of you?' The soldier, coughing up blood, spat defiantly in Chief Oko's face. In retaliation Chief Oko impaled his left leg. The soldier screamed in agony.

Seething, Chief Oko said to the soldier, 'You feel that, don't you? Good. The next one will be in your heart if you don't start talking. I want to know how many there are of you, and where are the rest?'

'*Você não pode me entender, mas em cinco dias vocês serão nossos escravos* (You can't understand me, but in five days you'll be our slaves).'

'What?' the chief responded. The soldier started laughing. But that was the last thing he did, as he fell dead.

Ade arrived with the rest of the Yoruba warriors. 'Are you three ok?' Ade asked.

They nodded. 'We're fine, Ade. Take the others into the huts and check on everyone.'

At that moment one of the chief's daughters ran out to get his attention: 'Father, come quick please.'

'What is it, Iyin?'

'It's Mum – she's been wounded.'

The chief's heart sank: 'No, not my Ayo.'

They ran to the chief's home. But when they got there all they could see was Ayo's lifeless body.

'No, no .... *NOO!!!!!!*' the chief yelled in agony. Femi and Dele looked at each other in despair; neither of them knew what to say. Chief Oko let out a tear; then another and another until an avalanche came flooding down his face.

Femi went to counsel Chief Oko. Chief Oko looked at him: 'How did this happen? You were meant to save us. You were meant to prevent this from happening.'

'I'm sorry, Chief, the Portuguese came earlier than I'd expected. I wasn't expecting your family to die.'

'I trained you, I trusted you. I was a fool to think you could help us. Now *get out of my sight!*'

Femi was disheartened by Chief Oko's words, but he knew that the best thing to do for the moment was to leave Chief Oko alone, so he left the hut. Soon afterwards Dele left as well, and ran to catch up with Femi.

'Femi, wait,' Dele shouted. 'This wasn't your fault. The chief's grieving. If it wasn't for you a lot more people would've died.'

'I know he doesn't mean it. For now he just needs space. Let's check on our fellow tribe members – Ade, I think, is going to need our help.'

'Agreed, Femi. There may be others who need us.' Dele and Femi went around the village to make sure everyone else was all right and to help wherever they were needed.

A day had passed and the dark cloud that had spread over the Yoruba tribe was still very much in existence. Everyone was shaken and scared, and didn't know what to do. Now they were mourning Ayo amongst other members. Femi felt bad for what had happened. He had been up all night staring into the wilderness, wondering what had gone wrong. He heard footsteps behind him and turned around. To his surprise it was Chief Oko.

'Femi.'

'Chief.'

The chief came and sat down beside him.

'How are you holding up, Chief?'

'I feel like a part of me has been taken away from me.'

'I can't even pretend to know what you're going through.'

'I am sorry for my remarks yesterday, Femi; that wasn't right. In honesty we would have lost many more if you hadn't stood beside me when engaging the Portuguese.'

'I was told that the Portuguese would come a year from when I first got here, though. It was said they would come with their entire army.'

'They still will, though, Femi. I sense that Oba Esigie may have had something to do with this early arrival. Perhaps somehow he knew that you were here and that you'd warned us of the coming threat.'

'But how, Chief? I thought Oba hadn't been seen or heard of in a few years.'

'Maybe he brought them with him.'

'Chief, what exactly happened with Oba to make him leave the village?'

'A few years ago a group of Portuguese explorers came to our shores. They were in search of treasure. Oba was hunting for food at the time and encountered them. He made a deal with them; he would lead these explorers to our deepest treasures and in exchange they would help him seize control of our tribe. Oba was very power-hungry and was always looking for ways to usurp me. The explorers in turn would have bled this land dry and enslaved my people. Fortunately we were able to deal with these explorers in time, and I faced Oba in a one-on-

one duel and beat him to within an inch of his life. I promised to spare him on one condition: he must leave Africa and never return here. He swore that some day he would return here to finish what he'd started.'

'Wow; that's some story. But how would he have made contact with these Portuguese?'

'He left with one of the explorers. In hindsight, I should have killed him. Now that mistake may cost us our village. We need to act quickly if we are to survive. Oba Esigie will have to be dealt with, but the Portuguese are a bigger threat. If only we knew when they're coming.'

'One of the things the soldier said was *cinco dias*; *dias* means 'days', and *cinco* 'five', if my language classes were correct,' Femi said.

'Well, whatever's supposed to happen in five days, it doesn't give us much time, Femi. I reckon these soldiers were just an initial few scouts sent to spy on us. We were lucky that their weapons made them so arrogant that they believed they could take an entire village by themselves. Their mistake has given us a break. And now we have an advantage, because we can guess when the rest will be coming. Ayo's death won't be in vain. Today we'll bury everyone we lost yesterday, then we'll avenge them by stopping the Portuguese. Your task here hasn't been completed, Femi; I need you. Are you still with me?'

'Always, Chief! I never left you.'

The chief offered his hand to Femi, and Femi accepted it to show that he still gave his support and to complete their reconciliation.

'Come now, Femi; we need to make preparations. After the burials we'll gather all the Yoruba warriors to discuss how best to tackle the Portuguese.'

The burials took place for the tribe members killed in the attack by the Portuguese. Normally in Yoruba culture a party would be held to celebrate the life of those who had passed away. This time, though, the circumstances meant that the celebrations would have to be put on hold. Burying his own grief, Chief Oko called an emergency meeting of all the Yoruba warriors to discuss their next actions.

Chief Oko addressed them: 'Yesterday was one of the worst days I've ever experienced in my entire life. We lost many that we hold dear. We grieve, we mourn and we honour their lives. But now is not the time to feel sorry for ourselves. The rest of the Portuguese army will probably be here in three or four days. We must be ready for them, otherwise everything we've built will be lost.'

'We need to mount a defence on the beaches,' suggested Femi. 'To enter this region everyone will have to land on the beaches. That's how I first got here. Ade, what do you think?' Femi turned around and noticed that Ade wasn't there.

'Has anyone seen Ade?' Chief Oko asked.

'Chief, I got this one,' said Femi. 'Let me go looking for him.'

He went outside and found Ade sitting by himself. Ade was caught up in his own world, and had forgotten that the briefing was starting.

Femi called out to him: 'Ade!'

Ade turned round: 'Oh it's you.'

'Is it ok if I join you?' Femi asked.

'Eh, come on.'

Femi sat down alongside Ade: 'How are you holding up?'

'I've had better days, Femi.'

'I can only imagine.'

'I doubt that. What do you know about loss?'

'I lost my father when I was four, Ade.'

'Oh sorry, Femi, I didn't know.'

'It's ok, Ade – it was a long time go.'

'It can't be easy losing your dad at that age.'

'It wasn't,' Femi said. 'Look, Ade, I know you lost your son when he was my age. He seemed like a great warrior.'

'Chief Oko told you, I'm guessing.'

'Yes. He told me before I took the first test in the mountains.'

'Femi, I know we haven't always seen eye to eye but I want you to know it was never personal. You see, in war you've got to go to the limit. You have to be ready to do what needs to be done with no hesitation, no mercy and no remorse. You need to be ready to kill in a blink of an eye, because your enemy will pounce on any weakness that you show. The moment you show fear you're as good as dead.'

'If that's the case, why are you so afraid to fight now? Me and Chief Oko need you now more than ever.'

'I'm not afraid, Femi. At least not what you think I'm afraid of. I'm not afraid of the Portuguese or their weapons. I'm not scared of death. The thing that worries me is what happened to my son. Having a son is one of the greatest privileges that a man could ask for. To have an heir to what you produce in your lifetime. To witness them growing up, getting married and having children of their own. This is a blessing. If we battle the Portuguese there are going to be many more fathers that will suffer the same fate. I wouldn't wish that on my worst enemy.'

Femi felt very sympathetic with Ade's state of mind. Ade often presented himself as being tough as bricks, and Femi wasn't used to Ade presenting himself as vulnerable.

'You blame yourself,' said Femi, 'for your son's death, don't you?'

'It was my fault. He wasn't ready. If I'd trained him better he wouldn't have died.'

'Oh come, Ade, that's rubbish and you know it. If your son hadn't joined the battle you'd have been killed, and the Yoruba tribe wouldn't be around today. You've concentrated so much on what you have lost that you've forgotten what you had. You didn't raise a man, Ade. You raised a champion, and one whose legacy will be told for generations to come. Many men have survived because of what you've taught them. If it wasn't for you, there'd be a lot more fathers and sons that would have been lost. Chief Oko respects you for a reason. Did you know that me and Chief Oko fought off a pack of lions whilst I was in the mountains? The defensive manoeuvres that I used were based on the drills you made me do over and over. You've saved a lot of men, Ade, and will continue to do so. But now is not the time for self-pity. We still need to stop the Portuguese. Not just for the Yoruba tribe. Not even for Africa. This is bigger than you and me. This battle is going to change the world. A lot of people are going to be saved from a life of hardship and torture when we succeed. But we can't do it ourselves. We need you with us, Ade.'

Femi opened up his hand and offered it to Ade. In a show of unity Ade shook Femi's hand.

'For someone so young, Femi, you speak truthfully. Thank you for reminding me that all of this is not for nothing. I'm guessing that you have an idea.'

'I do, Ade. But first we need to regroup with Chief Oko.'

Femi explained his plan to Chief Oko and the rest of the tribe. Femi knew that the Portuguese would have the edge on them in terms of firepower and manpower. So Femi's plan was to use fear and intimidation to make the soldiers lose their concentration, and make them easier to kill.

Femi's plan involved setting traps on the beaches to slow down the first batch of soldiers by impaling their feet. One of the other weapons that the Yoruba tribe used was a bow and arrow. Traditionally it was used for hunting. But this time Femi wanted to use archers to help take out the Portuguese. He wanted the traps to force the Portuguese into the middle of the beach. This would enable the archers to shoot fire arrows to help overwhelm the Portuguese and cut down their numbers. Femi also explained that to defend against the Portuguese firepower the Yoruba would have to add metal to their armour. Chief Oko was on board with Femi's plan, and the tribe set about making the preparations.

Everyone worked tirelessly to make sure everything was in place to repel the Portuguese. A few hours before the fifth day all the preparations were ready. Everyone in the Yoruba tribe had got into their positions. Now all they could do was wait.

'Are you sure this plan will work, Femi?' Ade asked.

'It will. It has to work. We *will* make it happen.'

Femi noticed that Chief Oko was on edge. 'You're thinking about Oba, aren't you, Chief?'

'Yes I am,' Chief Oko confirmed.

'What will you do if he's among the Portuguese?'

'Kill him. He had his chance.'

'I can see a sail coming up over the horizon!' shouted Dele from his lookout post. Femi took command and began laying down the instructions: 'The enemy's approaching. Everyone stay sharp.

Remember this day; it'll go down in history. Today is not just about avenging the people that we've lost. This is about making a stand. This is about us showing the rest of the world what the Yoruba tribe stands for. Today we fight for our motherland. Today we're going to show the world that no one's going to come to our land and enslave us. Now, are you with me?'

'*Yes!*' the warriors shouted.

'I said, *are you with me?*' Everyone shouted, '*YES!*' even louder.

'Good! Let's show these sons of bitches what happens when you screw around with the Yoruba tribe. Today they'll know that this is our home and that they can't take it. Now everyone, be on guard.'

Three ships eventually anchored just off the beach. The ships carried around 200 men each, so the Yoruba tribe would be outnumbered by around three to one. The Portuguese soldiers started rowing their boats towards the beach. They proceeded with caution, because it was a new land and they had no idea what was awaiting them.

Among the soldiers was a black person.

'Oba!' hissed Chief Oko, gripping his sword intently.

Femi said, 'Patience, my Chief, let him come to you. You always taught me to not let my options get the better of me. You'll have your chance. Together we'll beat him.'

'Now, be steady, archers! On my signal light your arrows and let them have it,' Femi commanded.

Meanwhile, the commander of the Portuguese army was saying to Oba, 'Our spies should have reported to us by now. Are you sure this is the right place?'

'Yes. I can recognise my homeland any time,' Oba replied.

The captain splashed onto the beach. After a brief look around he gave the signal to advance. The soldiers started to move inland across the beach. After around 20 minutes a crack was heard. One of the soldiers screamed in agony.

'Arrgh, it hurts, it hurts!'

'What is it?' the commander asked.

'There's something in my foot,' the soldier shouted, in severe pain. A few moments later he dropped to his knees, then fell to the ground and, in a few minutes, died.

The soldiers and the commander ran up to him, to find a sharp piece of metal stuck in his left foot. Shortly after, another soldier started screaming in pain. This was quickly followed by another and another. Soon around 100 men were suffering the same pains and dying the same way. The first part of Femi's plan had come to the fore. Each metal object was a piece of an *Iba* that had extra poison placed on it to make it even more lethal.

Fear and panic had begun to set into the heart of every Portuguese soldier.

Sensing an opportunity, Femi screamed, 'Fire! Make them burn and suffer!' The archers lit their arrows and fired them at the Portuguese. Many of them hit their target and the Portuguese numbers started to dwindle. The fire also helped blocked their vision and stopped them from having a clear view to shoot their guns at the Yoruba tribe.

Blood was being spilled and Femi knew now was the time to go in for the kill.

'Yoruba tribe, attack! Show no mercy, take no prisoners. Anyone not from our tribe dies today!' The Yoruba tribe charged at their enemy, and unleashed their full rage at the Portuguese. Driven on by the painful losses that they had suffered a few days earlier, the warriors were determined to avenge their fallen.

The Portuguese were overwhelmed. With their numerical and weaponry advantages stripped away, they found they were no match for the fighting skills and raw determination of the Yoruba tribe. The Portuguese had made a grave miscalculation with their initial onslaught a few days earlier; they had created a wounded animal seeking justice at any cost. Femi in particular held nothing back – he unleashed everything he had.

'This is for Ayo!' he yelled as he killed soldier after soldier with sheer ruthlessness.

Eventually Chief Oko caught up with Oba on the battlefield and engaged him in a rematch.

'Chief Oko! I told you I'd return. I always keep my promises.'

'And I told you if you ever returned here I'd kill you. Your anger and lust for power have made you betray your own tribe. Now you die!'

A ferocious sword fight followed. Oba and Chief Oko swung their swords viciously at each other, both determined to bring down the other.

Oba looked to have gained the upper hand and moved in for the kill. But Chief Oko threw sand into Oba's eyes and grabbed his right hand, twisting Oba's arm hard, dislocating his shoulder and making him drop his sword. Chief Oko picked up the sword and pointed it at Oba's face. Oba kneeled down, accepting his fate.

Chief Oko then spoke the last words Oba would ever hear: 'Know this; because of you Ayo died. Take that to your death. I showed you mercy once – a mistake that cost us severely. Now you die.'

Chief Oko thrust his sword into Oba's chest to the point where Oba could feel his life slipping away from him. As Chief Oko withdrew his sword, Oba fell to the ground and died.

Whilst Chief Oko had been fighting Oba the Portuguese had found themselves surrounded. They saw that this was a fight that they could no longer win. At first the Portuguese had had the advantage – they had the firepower, and they had outnumbered the Yoruba tribe by at least three to one. But what the Yoruba tribe lacked in men they had more than enough in terms of heart, spirit and willpower. The commander, looking around, saw that he was in no man's land. There was only one thing left that he could do.

'Retreat, retreat, retreat!' he ordered. The Portuguese soldiers left standing ran back to their boats.

The Yoruba tribe yelled out a massive roar: *Isegun* (victory), *isegun, isegun!*' they shouted in their victory pose.

Femi looked around at what he had been able to do. When he had first come to Africa and started his quest he had doubted whether he'd had what it took to truly change the course of history. Yet today he stood victorious with his people. Today he had achieved the first part of his mission. He had stopped the Portuguese from invading West Africa and in the process had saved countless lives going forward. Today he had changed the course of history!

Femi looked around and saw Ade, the man who had overseen his initial training and who Femi had not liked at all at first. Now, today, they had been fighting together like brothers. They smiled at each other and gave each other chest fist-bumps as a way of saluting the path that they had both travelled and how far they had come in terms of their relationship. A relationship that had started off with distrust on both sides had grown into respect, a respect that had since grown into brotherhood.

Ade started a chant: 'Femi, Femi, Femi.' One by one, everyone who had fought alongside them joined in. They gathered round Femi, lifted him up and paraded him on their shoulders. To the Yoruba tribe he had become more than a warrior. He had transcended into hero status. Whilst some had been prepared to give in when members of their tribe were killed by gunfire, he had never given up. He had stood up and found a way to beat the Portuguese at their own game. Now and forever more he had become a legend.

The Yoruba tribe celebrated well into the night. They danced and sang without a care in the world.

Eventually Chief Oko called everyone round: 'Today we mark a great victory. This victory will stand the test of time and it will be remembered throughout the ages. This victory isn't just a victory for the Yoruba tribe. It's not even a victory for the whole of Africa. This is a victory for the world. This is a victory for anyone that's been enslaved, for anyone that's been conquered, for anyone that's been attacked without due course. This is a victory for them.'

'*Beni, beni, beni!*' the Yoruba tribe shouted in agreement.

'But there's one man who we need to thank for making this day possible. And that's Femi Adebayo. When you first came to us you were a boy; you had heart and spirit but lacked the tools to fight among us. You went through hell with us, but you never gave in. You took whatever task and challenge that we threw at you and gave us back double in terms of effort. And when we needed it most you came to our aid. You gave us hope and were the light when darkness had descended on our tribe. For this we can never repay you. I don't fully know how, or understand where, you came from but as far as I'm concerned this tribe and our lands you can always call home forever.'

Femi was blushing at the chief's remarks. He was not used to receiving so many compliments. In response to the chief's kind words he said, 'Thanks, Chief. I couldn't have done it without all of your help.'

'I offer you more than a home and a tribe for life,' said Chief Oko. 'I never had a son until you came along. I'm offering you my youngest daughter, Iyin, in marriage. Also as reward for your bravery I offer you my crown as chief when my time to depart this world comes.'

Femi stood there shocked and surprised. This was not the scenario he had expected when he had come to West Africa.

'Chief Femi, Chief Femi,' all the Yoruba tribe shouted in approval of the chief's proposed successor.

Femi was happy, but he knew he had to turn down the chief's offer. 'I'd like to stay here forever. But I can't.'

Everyone was stunned. The people had grown to love Femi, and viewed him as one of their own.

'Please hear me out on this; my friends, my fellow warriors and fellow brothers and sisters. I came here as an outsider. My claims were outrageous to many of you when I first came here. Yet despite all of this you took me in and trained me. You made me into the warrior that stands before you today. For this you will forever be in my heart. Ade, when I first came here I hated your guts, and the feeling was probably mutual.'

Everyone started laughing.

'It wasn't personal, kid. I was just trying to toughen you up.'

'I know, Ade. You've been more than a trainer. You've been an uncle to me. And Chief Oko, if you were my father I'd have been proud to be called your son. The reason I can't stay here is not because I don't love or care for any of you. It is the opposite. My task is not complete. There are other people around the world who also need my help. There are other people who are enslaved or are about to enslaved, and I have a mission to put an end to slavery once and for all. I won't rest until slavery has been wiped out for ever.

'Also, the Yoruba tribe mission continues. The Portuguese or some other people like them will return in the future, so we must be vigilant. We need to spread the message to everyone else in Africa, and prepare them. We need to show them that slavery will not be tolerated. But now is not the time to dwell on the future. Now is not the time to be sad. For now, we rejoice, and enjoy what we've been able to accomplish. We've all won a great victory today, so for now we enjoy ourselves. Then tomorrow we will continue the mission to end slavery. So let's celebrate. *Isegun, isegun, isegun!*'

The Yoruba tribe joined in with Femi's chant and celebrated with Femi. The celebrations continued throughout the night.

***

Femi got up at dawn. He had now got so used to getting up at that time it was as if he was programmed to do it. He got dressed and took his armour and sword. He went back to the grounds of the gauntlet where he had cemented his status as a Yoruba warrior, and practised the fighting drills that he had learned whilst he was training. Dambe, Kokawa, Striking and Engolo; the African martial arts that would be adopted by many civilisations in the future.

He then picked up the *Iba*, and rehearsed the techniques that he had mastered under Chief Oko's tutelage. Head, left shoulder, right knee, left leg, backflip, guard pose. Right shoulder, thrust, thrust, roundhouse kick, bock right, bock right.

'For someone that had just led the Yoruba tribe to massive victory, anyone would think the battle hadn't started yet.'

Femi stopped and turned round to see the fatherly figure of Chief Oko waiting for him.

'Morning, Chief, I couldn't sleep. And I felt like training.'

'Understood; you need to head on with your journey.'

'I hope you're not too upset with me refusing your offer?'

'Upset? No, I'm sad to see you go, but your destiny lies beyond these shores.'

'Let me guess, you're here to offer me some final words of counsel.'

'You know me too well, Femi. May I?'

'Always, Chief Oko, always.' Femi put away his sword and went to sit down with Chief Oko.

Femi began to reflect on his time in West Africa: 'I've been on some journey here. I can't believe this has all happened.'

'We've all been on this journey, Femi.'

'I'm sorry I wasn't able to save your wife. I didn't know that was going to happen.'

'No need to apologise, Femi. In war you save as many lives as you can. Unfortunately that doesn't mean everybody. Ayo lived a good life and gave me and my children many happy memories. She died a happy woman with no regrets. If it weren't for you I might not have a kingdom left to defend.'

'I guess I can't save everyone. But it doesn't stop me feeling guilty about the people that I didn't get to save.'

'That's because you're a good man, Femi. You care deeply for your fellow humans. I don't know your family, but they – especially your father – would be proud of the man you've become. I only have one thing left to pass on to you, Femi. Fighting wise you've everything you need. Use what you've learned here. Practise the techniques and harness your skills. However, you won't be able to win this war alone. You can't do it all by yourself. Based on what you've told me, you're going to go away to faraway foreign places. So, surround yourself with people who you know you can trust and who will fight nobly for your cause.'

'How will I know who to trust, Chief?'

'Trust your instincts, Femi. In time you will learn to be good judge of character. Eventually everyone's character reveals itself. Do this, and I know you will be successful wherever you may be. Should you ever need help, know that the Yoruba tribe will always be on hand to help you.'

'I'm going to miss these pep talks, Chief.'

'I'll miss giving them to you, Femi.'

For the final time Femi and Chief Oko hugged and embraced each other.

'I have one final thing to ask of you, Chief.'

'Sure, anything,' responded Chief Oko.

'Remember my words yesterday about the mission of the Yoruba tribe not being complete? We need to spread the message all over Africa. Everything we've learned about the enemy needs to passed on to our neighbouring tribes and across borders. We need to make sure that Africa is protected for many years to come.'

'You have my word, Femi, that this will be done. Now before you depart you must stay and eat breakfast with us. I think there are many people that wish to say goodbye to you.'

'I will gladly eat with you all one last time.'

Femi went back to the village with Chief Oko. Everyone had gathered round to join Femi in one final feast. The breakfast was as a big a celebration as the one they'd had the night before. At the end of the meal Femi went back to his hut to gather his things, and prepared to head on his way.

The Yoruba tribe waited outside for him. When he went outside he was greeted by rousing applause.

One of the children approached him with some items: 'Femi, we made this for you. Please, this is food for your journey.'

'*Eshe* (thanks), little one,' Femi said then shook hands with and greeted as many people as he could before he departed. Eventually he saw Ade.

'Come here, you,' said Ade. He grabbed Femi and gave him a big hug.

'That's probably the nicest thing you've ever said to me, Ade.'

'You've earned it. Now remember what we taught you. You have many dangers ahead of you, so be careful. If you ever need us, know that we'll be here for you always. Good luck!'

'Good luck to you too, Ade.'

Femi took one final look back at the village and waved them all goodbye.

Then he headed back to the beach where he had first arrived in West Africa. Remembering the instructions that Mr Diggity had given to him, he said, 'It's time to go and save Nat Turner. *It's time to resume the mission.*'

Femi's time bracelet reappeared, with a glowing bead. He pressed the bead and disappeared into the time portal to head to his next destination. It was time for the next part of Femi's adventure.

Chapter 13: Where is Nat Turner?

Going through the portal, Femi found himself transported to West Virginia, USA, in 1832. According to the glowing bead, it was a few days before Nat Turner was due to be beheaded. On arrival Femi found that his attire had morphed into clothing of that period: black leather shoes, long pants, and a simple chequered long-sleeve shirt.

'Well at least I'm wearing shoes again,' Femi remarked to himself.

Looking around, he noticed that he was in woodlands. He began making his way through the trees. As he slowly moved forwards, he heard horses, so he decided to investigate quietly, to see what the horses were carrying. He silently snuck through the woods, and came across a spot which would enable him to see what was going on yet was dark enough to allow him to hide in plain sight.

'Let's see what we have here. Perhaps they can provide me with some information on where I can find Nat Turner.'

Femi remained vigilant but silent, and decided to observe what was going on.

As the horses came into Femi's line of sight, he noticed they were being driven by one soldier. Also the horses were pulling a wagon. Inside the wagon there were two soldiers and at the back of the wagon was a black man sitting with his wife and child. Both of them were in chains. The horses came to a standstill.

The two soldiers got out of the wagon, and one of them pointed his gun at the family: 'Move, niggas; I haven't got all day.'

Showing no regard for the baby the lady was carrying, the soldier shoved her along.

The husband began pleading for his wife. 'Please leave her alone; she only recently gave birth.' He got a punch in the face and a kick in the stomach.

'Did I give you permission to talk? Nigga, when I want you to talk I'll ask you to talk. Now get back up on your feet and move.' The man struggled back onto his feet and carried on walking.

Seeing this made Femi's blood boil. He clenched his fist tightly and was ready to unleash hell upon the soldiers. He was about to charge in, but taking stock of the situation he knew he was outnumbered. In addition they had guns and could kill him in an instant. He was desperate to rescue the young family, but he knew he had to be smart about this. He needed to be patient and wait for his opportunity.

The soldier who had hit the man told the driver, 'Wait here. We'll be back shortly.'

They went down a narrow pathway. Seeing this as the opening he needed, Femi decided to creep up on the driver. He crept up slowly and low so that he wouldn't be seen or heard. When he was within striking distance he put the soldier in a headlock and dragged him onto the ground. The soldier struggled for breath, but holding him tightly, Femi snapped his neck, killing him instantly.

Femi searched the soldier for weapons and any other items that might prove useful. He came across a map with a list of names and locations. He also took the soldier's gun. In addition he found that the soldier had a knife, ammunition and what appeared to be matches.

'Hmmm why do I get the feeling I'm going to need these matches later? Sometimes it's the least obvious items that make the most useful weapons,' Femi concluded. Once he had finished removing all the items that he could find he went down the pathway to continue his rescue mission.

Meanwhile the two other soldiers were busy tormenting the black family.

'You're going back to the farm. You shouldn't have tried to escape.'

'I'll never stop trying to escape. You might as well kill me.'

'Kill you, and lose out on profit? Now why would we ever do that? Now, get moving, nigga.'

A gunshot was heard. Everyone looked around, confused.

'Sergeant!' the second soldier yelled. As the sergeant turned round he could see blood running from the soldier's chest as he fell to the ground and died.

The sergeant grabbed his gun and looked around.

'You dare kill an army officer? Show yourself; you're mine. Now come out and fight me like a real man.' The sergeant found himself shot in both kneecaps.

'Ahhh!' he screamed as he fell to the ground, dropping his gun. Realising he was defenceless he reached for it, only to see a foot stood on it. The sergeant looked up to see whose it was.

Femi was there, standing over him: 'Hello, sergeant. We need to talk.'

Femi grabbed the sergeant by the throat and threw him at a nearby tree. 'So you think it's ok to call people *nigga*, huh?' said an enraged Femi as he punched him in the face. 'You think you're a tough guy because you pick on a defenceless woman, huh?' Femi bashed the sergeant's face again.

'Ahh, please stop!' the sergeant begged.

'So you'd like to talk, huh? Well, let's talk. Let's talk now.'

Femi ruthlessly pummelled the sergeant until he fell down and was on the verge of death. Femi stopped and stood defiantly above the sergeant. The sergeant was left begging for mercy, coughing up his own blood. Femi decided now was the time to get some information. Placing the battered sergeant against the tree trunk again, Femi started asking what he wanted to know.

'Right, I'm looking for Nat Turner; he was captured recently. Where's he been taken to?' Struggling to talk and gasping for air the sergeant replied, 'I don't – *cough* – know.'

Femi slapped him across the face: 'Give me another response like that next time and I'll rip out your throat. Now, where is Nat Turner?'

'I'm not telling you, shit nigga.'

'All right, have it your way,' Femi sarcastically replied. He began to walk away. The sergeant breathed a sigh of relief, thinking that he had been spared. As a somewhat sick joke and as a retort for the pain that the sergeant had been inflicting upon slaves Femi picked up his gun, turned round and blasted him in the forehead.

Femi for a moment reflected upon the carnage that he had just inflicted. He looked at the blood on the ground and his clothes. He hadn't set about this mission to become a murderer. In 15th-century West Africa Femi had killed, but it was always a case of killing to survive, and defending the village. But now in a moment of anger, he had unleashed sheer brutality and savagery in cold blood towards another human being.

Femi had sworn to follow the ways of a warrior that Chief Oko and Ade had placed on him. He was wary of going down a dark path and turning into the very evil he was supposed to be fighting. Before he had set out on his quest Mr Diggity had warned him about the depths that he might go to in order to complete his mission. The gravity of those words made him question what he was doing.

Whilst trying to make sense of what he had done Femi searched the sergeant he had just killed, and again, like he did the other soldier, stripped him of all useful items. He came across a pair of keys and a note. The note mentioned the county jail.

'These keys must be what he used to lock the slaves up,' he said to himself. He went to go and meet the couple. They had witnessed what Femi had done and were petrified.

'It's ok. I'm not here to hurt you. I've come to help. Here, I have the keys.'

Femi went on to unchain the family.

'Thank you, stranger; we would have been taken back to the farm if you hadn't shown up. I only have one question. Who are you?'

'My name's Femi Adebayo.'

'Hello, Femi, I'm Seun Beon. This is my wife Lisa, and this is my son Lleyton. He was born a few weeks ago.'

'It is a pleasure to meet you, Lisa. Many congratulations on your newborn child.' Femi shook Lisa's and Seun's hands.

'So why are you here? West Virginia is not a safe place to be right now, especially for a black person. That's why we were trying to escape.'

'I came here to rescue Nat Turner.'

'You mean *the* Nat Turner? He's the one who started the rebellion. And what do you mean by *rescue*? Has he been captured?'

'Yes. He'll be executed in a few days unless we rescue him.'

'We can't lose Nat. If he dies everything's lost.'

'I know, and that's why I need to find him. I've found there's a county jail nearby, and perhaps that's where he's being kept. If so, I'm going to bust him out.'

Seun felt Femi was being naïve, so he said, 'How? I mean what's your plan for rescuing him?'

'I'm not sure yet. I'll formulate a plan and make it happen.'

'Femi, based on what I've just seen you have incredible fighting skills. You've obviously had training. But this was only three soldiers. That, and you had the element of surprise. At that jail you'd be going up against a potential army. Even you can't take on the entire world by yourself.'

'You're right, Seun. I need to go and get my own army. I'm sure there are many slaves that would be willing to help me with this quest. If we free others there, many of them will help me. Do you know anywhere where we may be able to find some volunteers?'

'The farm we were about to be taken back to – there are many slaves there. If we can free them we may get the army you're looking for.'

'Excellent. There is only one problem; your wife and child. We need to keep them safe, and you as well. We can't get them involved in this conflict. First let's find them a safe haven.'

'Agreed,' said Seun. 'I'll take them to where we were escaping to. You can come back here at night and rescue everyone.'

'That sounds good to me. All right, Seun, lead the way.'

'Sure, follow me.'

Femi followed Seun to the safe house that he and his family had been heading for. Femi realised that he had found an ally in Seun. Femi smiled and said, 'Seun, is it me or does this feel like the start of a very beautiful friendship?'

'You helped rescued my family and me. For that I'll be in your debt for ever. Hopefully someday I can repay you.'

Chapter 14: Who wants to find Nat Turner?

Femi, along with Seun Beon, Lisa and their baby, eventually arrived at the safe house. There were two other people waiting for them: Lisa's brother Dylan and her sister Theresa.

'It's good to see you both safe,' Dylan said as he hugged his sister and Seun.

'It's good to see you too, Dylan.'

Dylan then caught a glimpse of Femi: 'And who is this gentleman, may I ask?'

'This, Dylan, is Femi. It's all right, you can trust him. Whilst we were on our way here we got caught by soldiers. Femi rescued us. If it hadn't been for him we'd be back on the farm.'

On hearing this Dylan shook Femi's hand and welcomed him with open arms: 'Thank you, Femi. Please join us. We don't have much, but we'll share what we have.'

'I appreciate your generosity, Dylan. We'd better get inside, though, just in case we get spotted.'

Dylan led them all inside. The safe house wasn't really a house. It was an abandoned factory, which had been burned down by a fire a few years earlier in an accident and was deemed unsafe for anyone to work in. So no one ever set foot in the place, which made it a perfect safe house for the fugitives to take cover from soldiers and slave traders.

'Theresa, please help Lisa with the baby. I need to go over the plans with Seun for tonight.'

'Of course, Dylan.' Theresa went off with Lisa to help find the baby some dry clothes.

'Is everything all set for us to leave for Canada?' Seun asked Dylan.

'Yes. Me and a couple of others have secured a boat that will enable us to get there. Then we'll go to the place where your cousin is staying. It seems to have better conditions for black people to live.'

'That's good news, Dylan. Good news indeed. When does the boat depart?'

'Tonight.'

'Tonight? That's soon.'

'If we wait any longer there's a chance we'll be spotted and then we'd be unable to leave this place. We have to take this chance to get out of here. We may not have another opportunity. Deputy Sheriff Edward Butts is preoccupied with Nat Turner, so no one will be watching the river banks. This is our best chance to escape.'

Seun replied, 'Very well, then. Tonight we leave.'

'Femi,' said Dylan, 'I've only just met you, but in our household we repay our debts. In return for helping Seun and his family you're very welcome to come with us to Canada to escape this nightmare.'

'I appreciate the offer Dylan, but I can't come with you.'

'Why ever not, Femi? I mean, what do you have to keep you here?' Dylan asked.

'Well, believe it or not I only just got here. What's keeping me here is my mission. I'm here because of Nat Turner.'

'Nat Turner! That guy was terrific. He really stood up to these sons of bitches. He helped lead the rebellion that freed many of us.'

'Dylan, you speak of Nat Turner as if he's dead.'

'He will be, once Deputy Sheriff Edward Butts is done with him. He's been trying to get hold of Nat for ages. Nat went into hiding after a battle went sour. He lost many men. He was discovered by some white farmer in the woodlands. With Nat, black people had a chance of standing up to this oppression. But without him we don't have any hope in hell. That's another reason why we need to get out of here.'

'There's still time to save him. That's why I'm here. I'm going to rescue him and get this rebellion back on track. The rebellion can still be a success, but we need Nat Turner to turn it around.'

'You're going to rescue Nat Turner? Ha! Dylan said somewhat amused by Femi's mission declaration. 'What are you? You're either brave, or you're stupid or maybe you're both. We all want to see Nat Turner live, but one man's not going to be enough to save him.'

'Exactly Dylan; that's why I'm going to raise an army.'

'An army; can you please explain where exactly this army's going to come from? You said it yourself – you've only just got here!'

'The farm that Seun and Lisa were going to be taken back to has other slaves. If we save them they may aid us in our mission.'

'This is insane! You're going to go back to the farm, kill any soldiers that might be in your way and rescue any slaves that they're holding, all in the hope that they may join you in this mission? And you're going to do all of this by yourself?'

'If I have to do it alone then so be it,' Femi said defiantly.

'You won't be alone, Femi, as I'll be going with you,' Seun said, interjecting himself into the discussion.

'Excuse me, Seun?'

'Femi, you saved my life. You've given my son a chance to have a life away from this. I've seen you fight; I know what you can do. But you're just one man. By yourself your chances of pulling this off are slim. But if you have me by your side, if you have someone that can watch your back, then this plan of yours may just work.'

'Seun, I appreciate the offer, but you have a family to consider. Your wife needs you. I can't guarantee your safety in this. Your son needs you. I lost my father when I was four, and I'm telling you from first-hand experience it's not an easy thing for a boy to grow up without his father.'

'If I don't help you, and let you plunge to your death, what kind of example is that setting to my son? I want my son to grow up to be a good man. Good men pay their debts; but most of all, good men stand up and can be counted on when they need to. Good men do this for one reason and one reason alone; because it's the right thing to do.'

Seun's words resonated with Femi. It also reminded him of the lessons that Chief Oko had taught him concerning what it means to be a true warrior. In Seun, Femi could see exactly the sort of spirit he would need to succeed in this mission. Despite his reservations, Femi gave in to Seun's request, saying, 'Well when you put it like that, I can hardly refuse. You can come on one condition. Your wife needs to be comfortable with this.'

'That's fair enough. I'll speak with her at once.'

But Dylan was furious with Seun. He was also worried that he would leave Lisa to raise his son by herself. 'Seun, you can't be serious. Think about this. You have a son, for crying out loud.'

'It is because of my son that I'm doing this.'

'You're both crazy. Femi, I'm counting on you. Make sure you return this man in one piece.'

'I'll do my best, Dylan.'

'You'd better, Femi, you'd better. Good luck to you both. You're going to need it.'

Femi asked, 'Dylan, you mentioned a man called Deputy Sheriff Edward Butts. Who's he?'

'Butts is the big chief around these parts. He was put in charge of rounding up the rebels and getting Nat Turner. He created a task force of soldiers and other lawmen to help him do his bidding. He also placed a $1,100 bounty on Nat Turner to encourage people to go out and find him. It was claimed by someone called Benjamin Phillips. If you're going up against Deputy Sheriff Edward Butts, he's a vicious, murdering psychopath. To beat him you're going to have to go to a really dark place. With him it's kill or be killed. Make sure you show no mercy, no hesitation and no remorse when and if you ever come up against him.'

'Thanks for the information. That was very useful.' Femi felt a strange sensation suddenly creeping inside him. For the first time in his mission he was afraid. Femi was afraid of what he would have to do to beat the enemy. He was worried that all the training that he had undertaken, instead of making him into a warrior had made him into a monster. Femi started to wonder if he had become just as bad as the people he was fighting against.

When night fell, Dylan prepared to head off to the boat to go to Canada with Theresa, Lisa and her baby. Meanwhile Femi and Seun prepared to go to the farm. They gathered their weapons and mentally prepared themselves for the upcoming battle. Before everyone departed, Seun and Lisa had a long cuddle and kissed each other goodbye.

'Be careful, my love,' Lisa said with a tear in her eye.

'I will. I'll see you and our son in Canada. I have to do this.' After a final kiss, they headed off to their points of departure with their companions.

After some time Femi and Seun reached the farm. They scouted around it to plan their attack.

'Ok, Seun, you know this farm. What are we up against?'

'When I was last here there were at least ten people patrolling it. The owner had hired some soldiers to help keep the slaves in line.'

'In other words, we can't go in all guns blazing. We need to bring them to us. We need a distraction.'

'I suppose you have an idea?'

'Well, there are these.' Femi pulled out the matches he had taken from the soldier earlier on.

He found a glass bottle on the ground, lit a match and placed it inside the bottle, then threw it as hard as he could. It landed just in front of the farm, the noise of breaking glass enough to alert the people inside.

'Why did you do that?' Seun asked.

'To get them to come outside We're still in the woods; we can use that to our advantage. We'll hide in the woods and pick them off one by one. No doubt they'll come here to investigate. Stay close to me and follow my lead.'

As expected, the soldiers came out. Inspecting the broken glass, one of the soldiers said, 'There's someone out here. Split up and check the place out. Bring the culprit to me.' The other five split up and started to prowl around the farm. They searched for about ten minutes and regrouped when they couldn't find anything.

'We can't find anyone,' each of them reported.

'Someone has to be here. Broken glass that is set on fire doesn't magically appear.' Gunshots were then heard, and two of the soldiers fell dead.

'It's the woods! The culprit's in woods. Go and find them. Go carefully. We're dealing with someone who's had some training.' The remaining soldiers slowly approached the woods looking to find whoever was responsible. As they went into the woods they split up and search individually.

Femi and Seun were able to pick them off one by one. A soldier fell into a small ditch that Femi and Seun had dug; the soldier's left leg got caught inside, and Femi ran out and slashed his neck. Another soldier walked past a bush where Seun was waiting. Seun crept up behind him and knifed the soldier in the back. With these two kills, only two soldiers were left.

As one of the two was walking deep into the woods he was spotted by Femi and Seun; they decided to use the shadows to confuse him. Femi quickly ran into the shadows in a direction that allowed the soldier to catch a brief glimpse of him. The soldier fired his gun furiously at the shadow but to no avail. As the soldier went across to try and get a close-up view of what he had spotted Seun ran into the shadows in the opposite direction.

Again the soldier got a brief glimpse of him and starting shooting, to no success. Slowly the soldier looked around helplessly; he stared into the wilderness and couldn't see anything.

'Where are you?' he shouted.

'Boo!' Femi said as he hit him from behind. The soldier fell to the ground, and Femi shot him.

There was only one soldier left standing.

'Hello! Is anyone there?' the soldier yelled, but received no response. He continued to probe further into the woodlands. He came across a pond and he saw a uniform jacket floating in it. Fearing it was one of his comrades, he ran over to the pond and picked up the jacket, only to find that it was empty. Seun tackled him from behind and made him drop his gun. As the soldier fell to the ground Seun repeatedly hit him. Femi came out from the shadows and placed his arm on Seun's left shoulder: 'Easy, Seun, don't kill him. We have a few questions to ask him.'

'I'm not telling you anything,' the soldier said.

'On second thoughts, hit him some more, Seun,' Femi responded.

'Is that it?' the soldier said as he started to bleed profusely from the mouth.

'All right, tell me, how many slaves do you have on that farm?' Femi asked the soldier.

The soldier remained silent.

'Are there any other soldiers on that farm?'

'I'm not telling you, shit nigga.'

'All right then, Seun, now you can kill him.'

'Kill me? No, wait ...' Seun shot the soldier at point-blank range.

'All right, Seun, let's go and rescue the slaves. But proceed with caution – we don't know who else is in there.'

Femi and Seun headed inside the farm, where they saw that the slaves were chained up.

'It's ok, everyone, we're here to get you out.'

'Over my dead body,' came a grouchy voice.

'Look out!' said one of the slaves. Femi and Seun dived for cover as shots were fired in their direction. They retreated behind the farmhouse door.

'Who the hell do you niggas think you are?' the voice said.

'I take it you're the owner,' Femi guessed.

'Damn right I'm the owner. I'm Farmer George. Now surrender or die.'

'You misunderstand our intentions, Farmer George. It is you who needs to surrender or die. We're freeing the slaves.'

'What kind of dumb arse nigga are you? Here you have no rights, here you work for me, here you ... heh.' One of the slaves stuck his leg out, tripping up Farmer George. Sensing the opportunity Femi and Seun leapt out in front of the door. Seeing Farmer George wide open they unleashed gunfire on him, killing him as he tried to get back to his feet.

Seun and Femi walked up to Farmer George to make sure he was dead.

Seun spotted the keys on him. 'Femi, look!' he shouted, pointing to the keys.

'Great, let's unlock them.'

Seun and Femi set about freeing everyone enslaved on the farm.

The slaves gathered outside. The majority of them didn't know what to do, and they couldn't believe their luck. In fact, for a fair few of them slavery was the only life that they had ever known. Femi and Seun gathered round them to address them.

'Hello, everyone. My name is Femi Adebayo. And this good man right here is called Seun Beon. You're all safe. You're not captives any more. You've all fought so hard to stay alive, and have lived lives that no one should ever have to live. You've suffered long enough, and you all deserve your freedom. You're all free to go. However before you do, there's a mission I'm on that may interest you all.'

'Go on, we're listening,' said one of the men.

'I'm on a mission to save Nat Turner. For a long time Nat has been the leading light against slavery in this part of the world, as I think many of you know already. But what some of you may not know is that he's been captured.'

'Nat Turner's been captured?' came a gasp.

'Yes he has. He's due to be hanged in two days. Without him the rebellion dies. But I have information on where he's being held, and I intend to rescue him. However, I can't do it alone – I'm going to need help. I know all of you have been through hell and I can't expect you to give any more than you've already given. This mission is going to be dangerous and I can't guarantee any of you your safety.

'In all honesty, I don't have a right to ask this of you. But if any of you still have the will to fight, if any of you still have a burning desire to see an end to this tyranny and if any of you are willing to go out there and fight the good fight one last time, I'd welcome your aid. No pressure; this is a choice that each of you needs to be comfortable making. I understand if you say no.'

The men began to look at each other and gesturing amongst themselves. Eventually one of them stood up.

'I'm Drake Moses. Nat Turner's been an inspiration to us all, and he's a reminder that we shouldn't accept our fate. If you're going on a mission to rescue him I'll gladly join you.' Drake Moses walked up to Femi and offered his hand.

Femi gladly shook it and welcomed his newfound comrade: 'Thank you, Drake. I'm glad to have you on board.'

'I wish to join you too. I'm Malcolm Ramirez. I'm going to be honest with you; I'm tired of the beatings, I'm tired of being made to feel like I'm worthless. If I go away now all that'll happen is some other slave trader will come along and enslave me again. But here we can make a genuine stand, and put an end to all of this once and for all. I too will gladly fight by your side.'

Femi fist-bumped Malcolm Ramirez to welcome him into the mission.

One by one all the captives stood up to join Femi. They were all sick and tired of running scared and feeling threatened. Femi looked at them all and gave each of them a nod of approval.

'All right, gentlemen. Welcome to the new rebellion. Now ... *let's go and save Nat Turner!*'

Chapter 15: Rescuing Nat Turner

Femi and his comrades spent the next day planning the rescue mission for Nat Turner. Femi began by restating everything they had learned so far.

'Ok. One sergeant who I killed had a note about a county jail. Maybe this is it. Nat's is going to be executed tomorrow unless we find him. Does anyone have any idea where this jail may be?'

'It has to be the county court jail. A lot of hangings have taken place there. I think that's where we should look,' said Drake.

'Then the county court jail's where we're heading tomorrow. We're going to need some serious firepower, though. This Edward Butts will have us outnumbered, so we're going to need something that'll give us the edge.'

'You mean something like those things over there?' Seun Beon said, pointing at something housed inside the barn. Femi and the men went back inside the barn. They saw a bunch of cannons.

'Cannons. Why would Farmer George ever need cannons? You can't milk a cow with cannons.'

Seun explained: 'Farmer George used to be a general in the US army. He sailed for duty in a raid as part of the US attempts to expand their influence overseas. US troops invaded parts of the Caribbean, which is why a lot of us ended up in the USA. But when they tried to raid Africa they got their arses handed to them.'

Femi paid close attention to Seun's last comment. Considering that when he had started this quest he had been in West Africa, he was intrigued to know more about the repercussions decades later.

'Why couldn't they invade Africa?'

'The Africans had put in measures to make sure no one could come to their continent to enslave them. It all began long ago when invaders from Europe tried to invade West Africa. They were Portuguese, I believe. An ancient warrior tribe held them off, inspired by an outsider. His example caused the African tribes to unite and help build each other's economies. An industrial revolution took place, and the Africans were able to build weapons that make these guns look like mere pocket knives. No one has dared try to invade Africa since. I hear Africa is now a paradise for black people.'

Femi smiled to himself. He was pleased to see that the African people had benefited from all that he had done whilst he had been there.

'I'm surprised none of you have tried leaving these shores and heading to Africa.'

'We have, Femi. But the government has put up blockades to stop us getting there. Our government is fearful of the power that Africa has. People in Africa tend to stick to themselves. Our government is fearful, too, that one day the Africans may decide to come over here and invade us. So keeping the border closed to us is their way of trying to stop us Africans from knowing about our world of origin, prevention being better than cure and all that.'

Femi, still smiling from this revelation, replied, 'Good to know; thanks for that, Seun.'

'Anyway, enough about Africa, Nat Turner's not going to save himself, is he?' said Drake, reminding everyone what their purpose was for coming together.

'Of course, Drake, you're right. We'll take the cannons with us. Tomorrow we'll unleash hell. The priority tomorrow is to save Nat at all costs. Anything that stands in our way, we take it down; we'll do whatever it takes.'

Drake suggested what they should do next: 'Femi, after we rescue Nat Turner we're going to need somewhere to hide. We'll need to regroup and think of our next course of action. We can't come back to this farm – it's one of the first places they'll look.'

'What about Organ Cave?' Malcolm asked.

'Where?' everyone asked. Organ Cave was unknown to almost everybody there.

'Organ Cave is a series of caves in Greenbrier County,' said Malcolm. 'The caves will give us protection and give us a safe haven to enable us to regroup once we've saved Nat. I heard about it from one of my former owners.'

'Sounds like a good option. Let's raid this farm and take away as many supplies as we can. We'll form two teams. All the women will head to Organ Cave to set up camp for us there. They'll be accompanied by some of the men, for protection. They'll head out just before dawn to avoid the soldiers. The rest of us will rescue Nat Turner and meet them at Organ Cave afterwards. Is everyone in agreement with this plan?'

Everyone nodded and was happy to follow through on Femi's plan.

'All right, let's get some sleep. We're going to need to be alert tomorrow.'

As the night went on, whilst everyone else was fast asleep Femi was struggling to get some rest. Eventually he got up and went for a stroll round the farmhouse, inadvertently waking Seun up. So Seun got up, and went to find out where Femi had gone. He found Femi staring into the woods, and joined him.

'Are you all right, Femi?'

'I'm fine, Seun.'

'Hmmm, I don't think so, Femi. If you *were* fine you'd have been fast asleep with the rest of us. We're going to need you tomorrow; you have to get your rest.'

'I've got a few things on my mind, Seun.'

'Tell me. Is it to do with the soldiers you killed when you first got here?'

'Yes, but it's more than that. For more than a year now I've been on a quest. I was trained in the ways of combat and I fought alongside the people that trained me, to help them stop an invasion. When I first started this quest I set out to liberate black people from slavery. I killed then, but when I killed it was to defend people. Since I've been here I have seen at firsthand what slavery has done to black people. I've only seen glimpses so far, but those glimpses were enough to make my blood boil. That, and the anger that I still have about what they did to my baby sister in my home city, really made me want to punish someone. Those soldiers were just unfortunate enough to be standing in my way. I guess I fear that I'm becoming what I set out to destroy. I came here to free the oppressed, but if I'm killing people without any regard for life, then am I really any better than men like Farmer George? This is a very dark path. I fear what I'm going to need to become in order to stop men like Edward Butts.'

Seun noted the confusion within Femi. He had appeared to be so strong and so in control that it was a shock for Seun to see him like this.

'Femi, listen to me. Everyone you've killed whilst you have been here – trust me! – had it coming. Those soldiers have treated us like animals. Some of them have tortured and killed us for sport, even. But *you* don't kill for the sake of it. You kill when there's no other option. You kill to save lives. If it wasn't for you I wouldn't be standing here, and my wife and child wouldn't be safely away from all of this. You've truly saved our lives. I have no doubt that your actions have saved other people's lives as well. You are an honourable man, Femi. Your quest is noble, and with you fighting alongside us we'll free Nat Turner and finish what we started. Remember why you're here, and you'll never fall into the darkness.'

'Thanks, Seun. I still feel that there may be another way to end this conflict. Something tells me that it's not going to be spilling blood that'll end it.'

'If there *is* another way, Femi, I believe you'll be the one to discover it.'

'If there is another way I'll need to find it quick. If only there was a way to reach out to people in Africa.'

'I don't think that's a possibility, Femi. They've deliberately locked themselves off from the outside world, and they treat all outsiders with extreme prejudice. It is a big reason why no one dares to try to invade Africa.'

'We need to get more allies,' Femi said. 'And that starts tomorrow, with Nat Turner. I've been looking forward to meeting him more than anybody else.'

'Me too, Femi, me too. He's a legend. It'll be good to meet the legend in person.'

'Let's get some sleep. We're going to need to be sharp tomorrow.' Femi returned to the barn with Seun a lot more settled in his own mind, and was able to enjoy a good night's rest.

At dawn everyone split into their groups to focus on their respective tasks. Femi's group prepared to rescue Nat Turner whilst everyone else prepared to set up camp in their new base. Femi's crew left for the county court as soon as they had gathered all the supplies they would need for the rescue mission.

Meanwhile in the county court Nat Turner was being walked towards the hanging area. Ever since he had been caught he had been beaten and tortured. He was suffering from malnutrition, too. Nat's plight delighted Sheriff Deputy Edward Butts.

'It's a nice day for this lawbreaking nigger to die. I've waited a long time for this. I'm going to savour every moment of this execution,' he said with glee. As Nat was being dragged to the assembly area, Butts emerged and stood in front of the crowd ready to witness the hanging. Butts had a speech prepared.

'Today marks a monumental victory for law and order in this country. Today we have a man named Nat Turner whose insidious crimes have resulted in the deaths of many innocent lives and whose rebellion has left a damning effect on our economy. Let this execution be an example to anyone else who is even thinking of rebelling against their masters. As is custom, I'm going to let the accused have a chance to say some final words. So, law-breaking negro, do you have any final words?'

Nat was silent. He had been beaten and broken. The famous fight and fire that had kick-started the rebellion had been extinguished.

'So, nothing to say, negro? Very well then, as you wish; you can die with your last words kept to yourself. Begin!'

The guards dragged Nat to the hanging area. They placed the rope around his neck. As they were about to lift him up to begin his hanging a chant was heard. Slowly the chant got louder and louder.

'What's that noise?' asked one of the lieutenants.

'I'm not sure,' responded Butts.

Then the words 'free Nat, free Nat!' could be heard.

When his army was within reach Femi yelled 'FIRE!!!!' Malcolm set the cannons off and unleashed their destruction on the surrounding area. They targeted the jail and the hanging area.

'FIRE!' Femi yelled again. Malcolm unleashed another round of cannon firepower upon the populace.

Panic began to set in on everybody. They screamed and ran for cover. Femi's plan was coming into motion and was being executed perfectly. Femi wanted to use the firepower of the cannons to cause mass panic, which would create a pathway to enable them to rescue Nat.

The lieutenant said, 'Sir, we must retreat and take cover.'

Butts would not be moved. He had been trying to capture Nat for months. He was determined not to let this opportunity slip through his grasp. 'I'm not leaving here until I see this man dead.'

'If we stick around *we'll* be dead! Let's go.'

Reluctantly Edward Butts retreated with his men.

Seeing this, Femi shouted. 'CHARGE!!!!.' and he and his men rushed in, killing anyone in their way.

They reached Nat, removed the rope hanging around his neck and released him from his bonds.

'It's all right Nat. We've got you,' said Seun. Nat, in a state of collapse, was carried away by Seun and Malcolm.

'We have what we came for. Let's move,' said Femi. Malcolm fired another round off from the cannons to aid their escape. They made it back to their horses and rode out of there to join the others in Organ Cave.

A weak Nat Turner whispered, 'Who are you people?'

'We're the new rebellion,' Femi replied. 'We've been inspired by what you've done for us, and we've come to rescue you. It's an honour to finally meet you, and I'm honoured to be fighting by your side.'

Nat, in shock and disbelief, fell silent.

The first part of Femi's mission in 19th-century West Virginia was complete. Nat Turner had been safely secured. But the hardest part was yet to come.

Chapter 16: Continuing the fight

Femi and his men found the camp set up in Organ Cave. It was a good hiding place, as due to the extensive underground system everyone could take cover deep within the caves should they be discovered.

Femi and his men begin to plot their next move.

'Right, now; we have three objectives. Our first is to get supplies. We need to get food, water and ammunition. We're going to be here for a while, and we need to make sure that we have enough.'

'Leave that to me,' said Malcolm. 'I know a nearby village. The village is filled with black people; one of the few such villages. We can fetch supplies when it's dark.'

'Thank you, Malcolm,' said Femi. 'Our second objective is to set up defences. We need a way of being able to detect if the enemy approaches, and to shield ourselves should we ever be under attack. Seun, you and a couple of the guys help set up some traps, and figure out a way to create some kind of alarm that will alert us to anyone that approaches.'

'I'll do so right away, Femi,' Seun said, and scampered away to get to work.

'Our final objective is to know our enemy. We need to try and find a weakness that we can exploit. Nat, whilst you were captive was there anything you discovered that we can use? Anything at all; even the smallest thing that we can leverage.' But Nat Turner, despondent, was sitting quietly in his own world.

'Nat!' Femi shouted. Nat finally came out of his torpor.

'Erm, yes, Femi, what is it?'

'Whilst you were captured did you spot any weaknesses that our enemy has that we can use?'

'Erm, not really, I don't know … I was too beat up to spot anything.'

'Nat, are you all right?'

'Yeah, look, I just need some space.' Nat walked away from the group and went further into the caves.

Drake had not been impressed with what he had seen so far of Nat, and he had no problem voicing his displeasure: 'This is Nat Turner. This is the guy responsible for killing many of our capturers. I thought he was a warrior. But this guy's just a desolate fool. It's like looking into an empty shell.'

'Give him a break, Drake. Nat's been through hell,' said Femi.

'We've *all* been through hell. But we're still here fighting the good fight. I didn't risk my life for some fake messiah. I thought he was the real deal.'

'Give him time. I'll talk to him. In the meantime let's begin our preparations.'

Femi went into the caves to look for Nat. Femi noticed that since Nat had been rescued he was very withdrawn. Femi was surprised at this, as history had denoted Nat Turner as a fiery preacher and the driving force behind the only slave rebellion successfully sustained in US history. Femi decided to try and understand what was wrong.

Nat, sensing someone was following him, shouted, 'Who's there?'

'Just me, Nat.'

'Oh it's you.'

'Can I join you, Nat?'

'Do as you wish,' Nat abruptly responded.

Femi approached him. 'You know, for a man who's just been saved from death you don't look happy about it,'

Nat, visibly frustrated, said, 'I didn't ask you to save me.'

'Ok, you're welcome. A little gratitude wouldn't go amiss.'

'Why should I show you any gratitude, Femi? What does saving me achieve?'

Femi was shocked at what Nat Turner was saying. 'Achieve? How do you mean?'

'I'm serious, Femi. Why did you save me? I mean, why are you here? What's your purpose in being here?'

'I'm here to stop slavery. Your rebellion is the key to that objective being met. The key to that rebellion is you. That's why I saved you.'

'I'm no key.'

'Yes you are, Nat. You've inspired a lot of people. Generations from now, people will hear about what you did, and be encouraged to stand up for what they believe in because of deeds such as yours.'

'My deeds are meaningless, Femi. In the end they achieved nothing.'

'Nat, I don't understand. Why are you being like this? What happened when they captured you? It's like they broke you.'

'I was broken long before they captured me, Femi.'

'Is that so, Nat? Broken men don't lead a slave rebellion that will go down in history as the most successful in the history of the US. Broken men don't provide hope and inspiration for the countless number of people they've helped. Look around you, Nat. Look outside. All of these men have risked their lives to save you. Are you trying to tell me all of this was for nothing?'

'Yes!' shouted an enraged Nat. 'All of this is for nothing. Don't you see, Femi? We can't win. No matter how hard we fight, no matter how hard we try, they'll beat us in the end. We're all going to die in the end.'

'So that's what's really bothering you. It wasn't the fighting, it wasn't being captured – it was being faced with your own mortality. For the first time in your life you were scared. Not because you were about to die. But because you were helpless to do anything about it.'

At that point a silence fell. Femi knew that he had hit a nerve. Nat turned away from Femi and went even further into his shell.

'Look, Nat,' said Femi. 'I'm not going to try to understand what you've been through or are going through. We all have our own battles and demons to fight. But I know this: outside of this cave there are a lot of men that believe in you. You started something special. I mean, look at where you came from. You were born on a plantation in Virginia. You were sold to slave traders three times in your childhood. That's no life for a child to live. My point is, despite all the things that you went through look at the man that you've become. You even learned to read and write, which not a lot of people who were born into slavery were able to do.'

'How do you know so much about my past, Femi?'

'Where I come from, Nat, your story has been told over and over again. It will continue to be told long after I depart this world. A good friend of mine once said that we can't change the past. But we can control the present and the future. You have another chance, Nat. You view yourself as having achieved nothing – but you've achieved something that very few people manage. You've become a legend. That's why all those men were willing to come and rescue you without any hesitation. Think about it. If they didn't believe in what you stand for, do you think they'd have followed me on what, to be frank, looked like a suicide mission? Well of course not.

We're all flesh and bone, Nat. At some point we'll die and our bodies will decay.

'However, before that time comes let's make our lives memorable. Let's make our lives *mean* something. You started a rebellion. Now let's finish this. You may have stopped giving a damn, Nat, but there are men out there that are ready and willing to kill for you in a second. We can't succeed without you, Nat. We need you.

'So there's just one question, Nat. What are you going to do? Are you going to stand up and fight, or are you going to drown in your own sorrows? Are you going to remind everyone of why you're a legend, or are you going to mope around and become a punk arse bitch? It's your choice.'

Nat's mood worsened: 'I can't hear any more of this crap.' And he stormed towards the cave exit.

'The truth hurts, doesn't it?'

Nat stopped walking for a moment.

'You know, when I first started this quest one of the people I was looking forward to meeting the most was you, Nat. I guess the saying's true where I come from: '*Never meet your idols. They won't meet your expectations and you'll just end up disappointed.*'

Nat walked out of the cave. Femi was stunned by what had happened. He had expected Nat Turner to be a courageous warrior. He had thought that Nat would be someone he would be glad to fight alongside and share the burden of his impossible quest.

But as shocked as Femi was, he knew he couldn't do this without Nat Turner. He had thought a few hard truths would have been enough to shake Nat out of his inertia. But that hadn't worked, so Femi wondered what else he could try. Then he felt a familiar presence nearby. 'Mr Diggity!'

'How did you know I was here, Femi?'

'Call it a gut instinct. I felt your presence.'

'Felt my presence! Since when did you become a Jedi? I thought West Africa taught you how to fight like a warrior, not develop a connection to a mystical force.'

'Mr Diggity, what's your obsession with Star Wars? The amount of times you throw a Star Wars reference my way.'

'Why wouldn't I? It's a great saga, Femi.'

'So is trying to end slavery.'

'Touché, Femi, touché.'

'I have a puzzle to solve, Mr Diggity.'

'I do like a good puzzle. Tell me more.' Mr Diggity crouched down next to Femi.

'What's happened to Nat? This isn't the Nat Turner you told me about. He led the most successful rebellion in US history. He was fearless. He was a preacher and a teacher, and didn't back down from anybody. But the man I see standing before me now is just a shell. Was history wrong about him? Was it a lie?'

'No, Femi, it wasn't a lie.'

'Then what's going on? I was expecting to follow his lead. I wasn't expecting to have to come here and lead this rebellion as well. That wasn't in the mission description for this part.'

'Why don't you want to lead it? You showed in 15th-century West Africa that you could step up and be counted on when people needed you! Why are you afraid to do so here?'

'I'm not afraid to lead if that's what's required. That isn't what concerns me. It's what happens afterwards. The reason for me coming here was to rescue Nat Turner. He has a big part to play in this mission if this rebellion is to be successful. It will inspire hope, and encourage slaves in other nations to stand up and rise against all acts of slavery. It was about lighting a spark that would burn slavery into the ground. Remember, I'm not from this timeline; Nat's the key. *He's* that spark. I just can't understand how he has changed so much. It's like he no longer believes in himself and his mission. It's as if he's lost his faith.'

Mr Diggity, acknowledging Femi's concern, said, 'I agree and understand completely where you are coming from, Femi. He *is* still the same person – history wasn't wrong about Nat Turner. The issue is he's been fighting his whole life. Like many black people of this era he was born into slavery. He has witnessed at first hand the worst of what people have had to endure in slavery. Let's also not forget that you rescued him from death.

'When you're close to death you think back about your life. You think about your mistakes, you think back to things that you never had a chance to accomplish, and you think about the people that you are about to leave behind. You also think about how your family and loved ones will survive without you. That's a lot to take on. Being on the brink of death changes people, I mean, how can someone not be affected by it? Imagine you've had something all your life then in an instant it's about to be taken away from you. Even if you do survive your ordeal it'll change your outlook on life.'

Femi reflected on what Mr Diggity had just told him: 'I never thought of it like that. I can't even begin to fathom what he's just gone through.'

'People's outlook can change for all sorts of reasons. Take those who have come out a life-saving surgery or lost a person close to them. Or, to a much lesser degree, a place you loved working in changed due to a new boss or a company direction. My point is that things in life can change quickly, and when those are changes that you didn't see coming it can take a while to adjust.'

'You're right, Mr Diggity. Nevertheless, we need Nat. I mean the real one. How do I get him back?'

'You need to have patience, Femi. Just like you've had to look deep within your own soul to get this far, Nat needs to do the same thing. Peace and happiness need to come from within. You can't force someone to be their normal self. Give him time, let him grieve and do what he needs to do to get back in the game. In the meantime, you're going to have to take point until Nat's ready to fight by your side again.'

Mr Diggity patted Femi on the back and got ready to head back to the future. 'By the way, Femi, I've been impressed with what you've done so far. You've exceeded my expectations on this mission. Keep up the good work.'

Femi smiled at Mr Diggity's compliment: 'Thanks. Do you know, you're the only person I know that can be perplexing and reassuring in equal measure? One minute you torture me, the next you're my biggest cheerleader. You're like a modern-day Jekyll and Hyde.'

'I know, Femi. It helps keep you on your toes,' said Mr Diggity, as with a flick of switch the door to the future reappeared. He walked through the door and disappeared. Femi pondered on the conversation he had just had and contemplated his next move.

Meanwhile back in the county jail area Edward Butts, still seething from Nat's rescue, was plotting his revenge: 'After four months of pursuing him we finally got Nat Turner and we lose him within, what, 30 seconds. How the hell does that happen?'

One of the lieutenants told Edward Butts some news: 'Chief, there have been reports of someone new on the scene. The person in question has been taking out members of our squad. He's rumoured to be saving slaves to build his own army in the hope of standing against us. In some quarters it's being called the new rebellion.'

'So, a new rebellion, huh! Whoever this new guy is, he has the gall to oppose *me*. How dare he? How dare he? I want him found immediately. This is unacceptable. I want this threat eradicated immediately. Search from pillar to post. No rest until these bandits are found. I'll skin 'em all alive for this.'

'Yes, Chief.'

Chapter 17: Preaching to inner turmoil

Femi regrouped with the rest of the new rebellion as they began to plan their next action. They knew that their hiding place would be discovered soon enough. In addition, the rescue of Nat Turner would only increase the bloodlust of the slave owners.

'We need to figure out how we're going to survive the next onslaught. Butts will no doubt double his forces to try and find us,' Drake warned the group.

Malcolm, meanwhile, was getting doubtful – he had seen a lot of blood spilt and was beginning to tire of the mindless killing cycle they were in. 'It's is no use, Drake,' he argued. 'I'm pleased to have Nat back alive and well, but for every white man we kill they'll send a hundred more. Even if we killed every white man in Virginia, they'd get reinforcements from Washington or nearby states.'

'Well, we can't just give up. Many of our people have died. There are still many of our people stuck on slave farms working their arses off for some son of a bitch that would happily whip them for no reason. And all for what? Just to extend the white man's empire! I don't think so.'

'So you'd rather continue to fight the endless armies of the white man with no end in sight? We might as well commit mass suicide.'

Malcolm and Drake bickered for ages. Neither man refused to back down. Femi listened carefully to both of their views, and after much deliberation he decided to intervene.

'You're right – *both* of you are right! There are many of our people whose lives have been lost in this war. Make no mistake, this rebellion is a flat-out war. There are also many of us who are still slaves and need our help. We can't abandon them when they need us most. But we can't continue to fight wave after wave of armies, either. That's only going to lead to our downfall. We can't help our people if we're all dead.'

'So what are you proposing?' asked Drake.

'We need allies. We need an army of our own. We need to form strong allegiances with people that believe in our cause. Now I urge each of you to think back to all the people you've met in your lives. Is there anyone else you can think of that would be willing to fight on our side?'

Reflecting on Femi's counsel, everyone thought deeply about who they could recruit. But more importantly the group thought deeply about who they could trust. The group went into a reflective silence.

Eventually Seun Beon broke the silence. 'I may know someone …'

Sensing Seun's hesitation, Femi said: 'Sure, Seun, go ahead. Don't be afraid. Who do you have in mind?'

'His name is Thomas Jackson.'

'Thomas Jackson? Who's he?' Malcolm asked.

'He's a general in the US army. But before his time in the army he used to work at a mill in West Virginia. He still goes there from time to time, to check on his half-uncle.'

Malcolm, not impressed by Seun's suggestion, said, 'Why would a US general be willing to help us? He's one of the enemy.'

'Simple; my elder cousin Nicholai Beon taught him to read. Later, Jackson helped him flee to Canada, and my family went to Canada to join Nicholai. I'll follow suit when we've sorted things out here.'

His revelation stunned the group. Many of them had only experienced negative actions from white people, so it was the first time that they had heard of a white person helping them freely.

'It's a very long shot, but Thomas Jackson's military connections may end up proving invaluable. Your cousin's history may convince him to join us. I think we need to go to this mill to seek Jackson's aid. We'll travel at night to avoid being caught. Does anyone have any objections?'

'I do!' Malcolm objected furiously. 'White men are the reason why we're in this situation. This Thomas Jackson can't be trusted.'

Femi, trying to relieve Malcolm of his concerns, said: 'Malcolm, I understand your reservations. But I see little alternative. We can't just keep going down the same path. Our pride mustn't get in the way of our survival.'

'But to trust some blue-eyed devil, sorry, after all they've done to us! And not just the here and now, but the centuries of abuse.'

'We're not asking you to trust Thomas. We're asking you to trust me and Femi. We have to try,' Seun interjected.

Malcolm was still seething with anger over the idea of asking Jackson for help, but he eventually relented. 'Seun, I've known you for a while. Your positivity was very often the only light we saw whilst we were working on the farm. You always said that one day we'd get a better life. And Femi, you've kicked off this new rebellion and given us a fighting chance. I trust both of you with my life. If this is what you think we need to do to survive, then so be it.'

'Thank you, Malcolm. Does anyone else have any other objections?' Femi asked, hoping that now everyone would be willing to give this plan a chance. No one else in the group raised any concerns about asking for Thomas Jackson's aid.

'Then it's settled. When nightfall comes, me and Seun will go off to Jackson and ask for his help.'

'Tread carefully, Femi and Seun. The soldiers will be looking for you. If they catch you they'll most likely kill you on sight,' Drake said.

'We will. We'll be back to continue the fight alongside you all,' Seun promised.

With consensus achieved, the meeting ended. Seun and Femi began their preparations to try to recruit Thomas Jackson to their cause. At nightfall, they set off on their journey. To avoid capture they decided to travel by boat; the mill was located just off the Hackers Creek river.

Close to midnight Seun and Femi reached the landing point. Once they got ashore Seun said they would have to pass through the woods to get to the mill.

'Ok, Seun, lead the way.'

After five minutes they arrived outside the mill.

'This is it, Seun?'

'Yes it is, Femi. Let's go and find him.'

'Wait, Seun.'

'What for?'

'We don't know if he's even at home. Let's not forget that technically we're fugitives. We can't risk anything until we know for sure that Jackson is there. We'll move in when we know for certain that he is.'

An hour passed and there was still no sign of Jackson. Seun, becoming restless, started pacing up and down.

Annoyed, Femi said, 'Seun, control yourself; if you carry on like this you'll give away our position. There's too much at stake for us to just charge in.'

'I know, Femi, but it's irritating just waiting here and not doing anything.'

'I know; I want to get this over with, too. But we have to be smart about this.'

At that very moment the front door to the mill started to open.

'Seun, fall back; I think I see movement.'

Seun crouched behind the trees, and waited anxiously with Femi to see who was going to come out. To Seun's joy it was Thomas Jackson. He was heading to the barn.

'Ok, that's him, said Seun.

Okay, we'll approach but slowly and carefully. This task requires stealth. Got it?' Seun nodded in agreement. Carefully Seun and Femi headed over to the barn.

Jackson was refilling some buckets to get water. He thought he heard a noise and turned round to see what it was. 'Who's there?' he asked. He waited but got no response. He thought he must have misheard and continued to fill the bucket.

A moment later a gun barrel pressed against his neck, and he heard the words, 'Don't move. I don't want to hurt you, but if I have to I will.'

Thomas stuttered, 'Who … who are you?'

'My name's Femi Adebayo.'

'Femi who?'

'Who I am is irrelevant. That's not important. Now you're going to listen, or I'm going to fill you with a load of bullets.'

'All right, Femi, you've made your point. What do you want?'

'I need your help.'

'Excuse me, Femi?'

'You heard me the first time. I need your help.'

'You come here in the middle of the night, disturbing my peace in my own home and threatening me. Give me one good reason why I should help you.'

'A storm is brewing, General Jackson. Too many people have died, and too many people are going to die. Both black people and white people have died. This is only going to get worse. Eventually a civil war is going to break out that will convulse the United States. I need your help to stop this from happening. Plus I also have someone I think you need to meet.'

Femi lowered the gun and allowed Thomas Jackson turn around and see Seun Beon, who was waiting for him.

'Hello, Thomas. I'm Seun Beon.'

'Seun Beon. As in ...'

'Yes I'm his family. I'm his cousin.'

Jackson was amazed at this revelation: 'Well I'll be damned! Your cousin was a good man. I was glad he managed to escape from all of this. Is he all right? Is he still alive?'

'He's well.'

'Ok gentlemen, you have my attention. What help do you need from me?'

'It's about Nat Turner ...' Femi began.

'That criminal; what about him?' Jackson interrupted.

Femi sensed that Jackson would not be easily swayed. Femi tried to reason with him: 'Sooner or later people will find him. One of two things are going to happen. If they find him they'll try to kill him. Or he'll kill them instead. Whoever dies, there will be repercussions, and the whole thing will be repeated again. It is just an endless cycle of violence. At the end of it all, what will have been achieved? It'll just result in a mindless and bloody civil war. I'm offering you the chance to help end this cycle. Fight with us and build a better tomorrow for everyone.'

'You want me to fight alongside you?'

'You're a respected man, General Jackson. You have army divisions you can call upon. People will listen to you.'

'Wait a minute! I heard that Nat Turner had been rescued. You must be the people that did that. I should have you arrested immediately for treason.'

Femi, disgusted and angry, raised his gun and aimed it at Jackson's head. He was very close to pulling the trigger.

'Go ahead, kill me. There'll be others,' Jackson said, egging Femi on.

But Seun, a voice of reason, said, 'Femi, think about this. This was not part of our mission.'

Femi's finger hovered on the trigger. At the last moment he relented.

Jackson breathed a sigh of relief: 'It looks like I'm not the only one who doesn't want to go to war. I may be a general, but for me war should always be used as a last resort. I only fight when there's no other option. Nevertheless, Nat Turner and his followers are hardly innocent. They too have a lot of blood on their hands. It's one thing to kill those who made you a captive or those that have enslaved you, but they've killed people that had nothing to do with them being enslaved. I can't ignore that, Femi.'

'You're right, General Jackson, sir. We *have* made mistakes along the way. But let's look at what led to all that happening. Imagine you were born into a world of slavery. Forced to work in unclean, unsafe conditions and being whipped when your work's deemed not good enough. Imagine living with the pain of your ancestors being in chains and being removed from their homeland without any say in the matter. Imagine living a life without choice or freedom. A life where you are treated as a lesser human being – treated worse than a dog! Imagine all of this happening to you all because of the colour of your skin. Imagine that, and multiply it by a hundred. That's what we've been going through for centuries.'

Jackson stood there silent. He didn't know what to say in response to Femi's claims. Jackson was genuinely stunned. He began to wince and reflect on the horrors that black people had gone through over the years. A tear arose in his left eye.

'Even if I wanted to help you to make this right, to help a wanted criminal is a felony. I'd be court martialled and stripped of my rank,' he asserted.

'It didn't stop you helping my cousin before. You knew it was the right thing to do then. You may be a white man, but you're a good man. My cousin knew this. That's why I said we should come here,' Seun said.

'I'm sorry. I wish I could do something, but I can't. I have sympathy for your people's plight. But there is nothing I can do,' said Jackson.

'I understand. If you do change your mind, you'll find us at Organ Cave.'

'What makes you think I won't give up your location to the authorities, Femi?'

'Nothing. I guess I just have to trust you.'

Femi and Seun left the barn. They began the long journey back to the Organ Cave empty-handed.

'What do we tell the others, Femi?'

'The truth, Seun. We tried. We soldier on, and we find another way.'

Chapter 18: The final stand of the rebellion

Although several weeks had passed, Butts and his men had not yet found Nat Turner's hiding place. But eventually they came across Greenbrier County, and received reports that a group of slaves had set up camp in the area.

Butts decided to investigate, in case it was the new rebellion's hiding place: 'All of this time and I still haven't found these bandits. How hard is it to find a group of slaves?' he moaned.

One of Butts' men gave his view on why they had failed to find the new rebellion: 'The problem is that they've inspired other slaves. Everyone we have interrogated so far won't give us any information on them. They're being protected, and it's making our lives more difficult.'

'We'll find them soon, lieutenant. Sooner or later they'll slip up.'

'Chief, I may have found something.'

Butts got off his horse to inspect what the soldier had found: 'What is it?' he asked impatiently.

'If I'm not mistaken these marks look like the tracks of a cannon.'

'A cannon? Of course! They used cannons to get to Nat. Which way do they tracks go?'

'They seem to lead this way.'

The soldier continued to walk in the direction of the trail. But a few steps further on he stepped into a hidden alarm. This triggered a chain reaction, starting a set of connected bells ringing.

Butts said, 'This has to be the work of the rebels. They must be close by. Let's move!'

When the sound of the bells reached the Organ Cave, Seun said, 'We've been found!'

'How on earth did they find us?' Drake asked. 'We've been so careful.'

'It doesn't matter how,' said Femi. 'We need to get ready. Prepare the men; we need to get into battle mode. Take the women to the hiding place as planned. Let's move!'

'We're on it, Femi,' replied Seun.

A mad dash followed. The members of the new rebellion grabbed their weapons and got into their battle positions. Femi asked Seun to get a close-up view on who they would be up against.

'It's Butts. He's here, and he's not alone. He's brought an army company with him.'

'How many men does Butts have, Seun?'

'I make it around 200 to 250, Femi.'

'That's not so bad. Malcolm, the cannons: how much ammunition do we have left?'

'Just three more rounds, Femi.'

'Then we'd better make them count. This is the end. We've battled long and hard to get this far.

This may be one battle too far. Gentlemen, it's been an honour fighting alongside you.'

There came a new voice: 'Don't be so quick to assume defeat, Drake. Where there's life there's hope.'

Everyone turned round, to see a mysterious figure emerge from the shadows. It was none other than Nat. Well fed and well rested, he had isolated himself from everyone to get his mind right and he was finally ready to take up the fight again.

'I thought this was meant to be the new rebellion,' he said. 'We've started something beautiful here. Thanks to you, our people have something to fight for. Butts is here because he's afraid of us, and this is the reason why he has brought so many soldiers. Well, I say let's send these bastards straight to hell. Now, are you with me?'

All the members of the new rebellion shouted a resounding *YES!*

Femi shouted loudest of all, then, 'Welcome back,' he said as Nat approached him.

'I didn't go anywhere – not physically, anyway. But I had some thinking to do up here,' Nat responded, pointing to his head.

'Any ideas on how what we can do to survive this?' Femi asked.

'We need to tweak our positions,' said Nat. 'We're a little bit too open. But we must hurry, as the enemy's approaching.'

After some last-minute adjustments Nat took up his position next to Femi. Along with the rest of the new rebellion they waited for Butts and his men to come into range.

'So it all comes down to this,' Nat remarked to Femi.

'Indeed it does, Nat; this is where we make our last stand,' Femi responded.

'Before the fighting begins I have something that I need to get off my chest. I may not get another opportunity. It's about when we were in the cave before. I wanted to say sorry for barking at you.'

Femi lowered his weapon and turned round to face Nat.

'Look, Nat, I'm sorry too. I wasn't thinking right. I was so focused on the mission that I wasn't being sensitive to what you'd just gone through. I mean, you'd been seconds away from death.'

'I understand, Femi. This life that we're living – being born into slavery, putting up with being called a nigga every other day, the endless fighting and killing – when you're on the verge of dying it does make you evaluate your life. It makes you question why you're doing what you're doing.'

'So what made you get back into the fight?' Femi asked Nat.

'Simple. I *had* to be in this fight. There are certain things in life that you have to do. You don't do them because you want to. You don't do them because you enjoy them. You do them because there's no other choice. You do them because the consequences of your inaction will lead to a situation that brings disparity to everyone. And not just the people of today, but the people that will one day grace this world when our flesh and bones are buried deep within the ground.'

'That's some deep shit, Nat.'

Nat, smiling at Femi's comment, responded, 'It's always deep when we talk about the real things. This is the stuff that really matters. But on a serious note, you saved me. You gave me another opportunity. Thanks to you I can help finish what we started.'

'Whatever happens, Nat, it's an honour to fight by your side.'

'Likewise, brother Femi, likewise.' Nat extended his hand to Femi; Femi gratefully accepted and gave him the brotherhood handshake. The two men knew that they had each other's backs and were in this together till the end.

After an anxious wait they saw Butts and his men marching towards them in Organ Cave. The troops stopped a few hundred feet away from the entrance, and Butts emerged from the pack to address the new rebellion.

'For those of you who don't know me, my name is Edward Butts. I'm the Deputy Sheriff, and I run this yard. For months I've been pursuing a criminal called Nat Turner. He's committed unspeakable crimes against the state. Justice was about to be done when your so-called new rebellion rushed in and rescued him.

'Nat Turner has a debt to society that needs to be paid. So I'm going to give you all two choices. We can do this the easy way or the hard way. The easy way is you hand over Nat Turner; the rest of you will then be allocated new masters to enable you to continue your great service to this country. Or we can do this the hard way; we'll come into this cave and take Nat Turner by force. Anyone standing in our way will be killed. Everyone we find will be beheaded and skinned to serve as a reminder to anyone who even *thinks* about rebelling against their masters. The word 'rebellion' will cease to exist. The choice is yours. Now make it snappy. I haven't got all day.'

The members of the new rebellion looked at each other, not knowing how to respond.

Nat decided to be the one to reply; 'I got this. Hey, Edward Butts, you sanctimonious bastard, who the hell do you think you are? You call yourself a lawman, yet for years you've let my people be victimised, whipped without mercy, raped, and you looked the other way the whole time. You're not serving justice. You're serving slavery. We're not standing for it any longer. If you want me, come and get me – if you dare, you coward.'

'YEAH!' the members of the new rebellion roared.

'Then so be it. The hard way it is. Men, advance! No prisoners. Kill them all!' ordered Butts.

As they started moving towards the cave, Nat gave the signal: 'All right, Malcolm, let 'em have it!'

Malcolm lit the remains of the gunpowder, and fired the cannons for the last time. The impact of the cannons gave the new rebellion some breathing space.

'All right, everyone, pour it on,' Nat Turner commanded. 'If this is the end, we'll take as many of them as we can to the grave with us.'

'You heard the man; let's end this,' Femi added.

The new rebellion's final stand was under way. Round after round of gunfire was unleashed by both sides. For a while the new rebellion was able to hold their own, until a disaster occurred; Seun got hit in his left shoulder.

'SEUN!' Femi shouted in despair as he saw his friend fall to the ground in pain. Other members of the new rebellion were also starting to be picked off.

'Fall back, fall back,' Nat instructed. Femi helped Seun get back onto his feet and fall back with the others.

Butts saw the retreat and knew that he had the new rebellion right where he wanted them.

'We have them, men. The new rebellion's finished. Go into the cave and polish them off.'

'This is it, isn't it?' Drake said. 'We did well to get this far.'

'Do you regret not walking away when I gave you the option back on the farm?' Femi asked him.

'Never! I got to see the real Nat Turner!'

Nat gave a wry smile. 'We're not dead yet, gentlemen. Let's go and get us some one last time.'

'Hear, hear,' Malcolm responded as he reloaded his rifle.

The new rebellion went to re-engage Butts' men. But as those men were about to enter the cave ten of them fell from by gunfire that had come from somewhere else.

Confused, Femi asked, 'Ok, what just happened? Who shot those men?'

'It wasn't any of us,' Malcolm said.

'Look!' Nat said, pointing to the hills. Another army unit was heading towards the cave. It was Thomas Jackson. He had recruited some former comrades and persuaded them to come to the new rebellion's aid. Edward Butts was not popular amongst some of the army; many soldiers had grown tired of how he treated people, white or black.

'Follow me to victory!' Thomas Jackson commanded, as his recruits helped turn the battle in favour of the new rebellion.

With their numbers enhanced, the new rebellion fought back with Jackson's men and pushed Butts' men back.

'We must retreat at once! We must ...' but at that moment a bullet came flying right through his chest. Butts put his right hand there, and when he looked down all he could see was his hand covered in blood. He looked up to see who had fired the fatal shot – it was none other than Nat Turner. Nat's face was the last thing Butts saw as he collapsed and died.

'About time I killed that son of bitch,' Nat Turner grinned.

Against all odds, the new rebellion had won. Femi's gamble had paid off. The unlikely alliance had saved the day. The men of the new rebellion shouted in joy to proclaim their victory. Femi and Thomas Jackson caught a glimpse of each other amidst the celebrations. They silently nodded to each other, signalling their approval and respect for the other man.

After the battle and when everyone had taken care of their wounds, Thomas Jackson, Nat Turner, Femi, Seun Beon, Drake Moses and Malcolm Ramirez got together. A glorious victory had been won – but now the way forward was unclear.

'Many lives have been saved by this. Not just today but in the future as well,' Nat proclaimed. 'However, our task is still not complete. There are still many people out there who have been enslaved. We have many battles to fight.'

'My men and I will be by your side to help you with whatever you need,' said Jackson. 'I know that in the past that we have not treated black people well. We have committed unforgivable sins. But I hope you will give us the opportunity to make things better for the future.'

In the past Nat would have rebutted such an offer, as he viewed all white people as being the same.

Jackson's actions, however, had opened his eyes to the possibility of peace.

'You made a great sacrifice to help us. Without your aid none of us would be standing here today. We'd all be dead. You've earned the chance to gain our trust. Together we can make a better future.'

An excited Malcolm asked, 'So, where do we start?'

'I think we should all march to Washington,' Thomas suggested. 'We'll go there in peace, and fight for the rights of black people. We'll pass a new Act – the Anti-Slavery Act. We'll ensure that, going forward, black people are treated the same as everyone else. No one will ever suffer again because of the colour of their skin.'

Malcolm nodded in approval: 'I like that. I like that a lot.'

'Sounds to me that you guys have this all figured out,' Femi pointed out.

'*You guys*. What about you? You're a part of this. You're part of *us*,' Nat replied, puzzled by Femi's comment.

'My task here is done. I came here to free you and restart the rebellion. Together we've done something even better. We've created the foundations for peace and harmony that will save an entire generation from the horrors of civil war. Plus my mission's not yet finished; there are other people around the world that need my help. It is time I got going.'

Everyone pleaded with Femi not to leave.

'You can't go, please don't leave! We *need* you,' Malcolm insisted.

'I'm honoured and touched that you wish me to stay. But I need to get going.'

On that note Femi offered Malcolm his hand to say goodbye, but Malcolm grabbed Femi and hugged him instead.

Femi went up to Drake and hugged him as well: 'You're one of the greatest people I've ever had the privilege of knowing. Goodbye, my friend.'

'Goodbye to you too, Femi.'

Femi then went on to hug and say goodbye to Seun. Tears rolled down from Seun's eyes.

'You have a good heart, Seun,' said Femi. 'Make sure you stay the same, no matter what happens in the future.'

'Yes, Femi,' Seun replied, as tears continued to flow down his cheeks.

Thomas was next in line. After hugging him goodbye, Femi asked him, 'So you did change your mind after all. What made you do that?'

'Something you said back in the mill about doing the right thing. Sometimes doing the right thing for the greater good is more important than rules, regulations and titles. A good soldier saves lives; simple as that.'

Femi nodded in approval of Thomas's answer.

Finally the historic figure that was Nat Turner stood before him. As they embraced for the final time, Nat thanked Femi for everything he had done: 'Thank you for bringing me back from the dead.

And by that I mean both physically and mentally. It's been an honour fighting by your side.'

'The honour was all mine, Nat. I'll see you in the future.'

Femi gave his comrades one last goodbye wave and set forth on his next mission. When he had got far enough away and was certain there was no one else around, he quietly said '*It's time to resume the mission.*'

His time band appeared, with the third bead glowing. Femi tapped on the bead and walked into the time door that materialised before him.

'Let's go and get these fools that are stinking up the Fredensborg,' Femi proclaimed as he was being transported to his next destination. He was at the halfway point through his mission. His next adventure was just a time tap away.

Chapter 19: Aboard the Fredensborg

For the third time in his mission Femi was transported through time. This time he would find himself in 1768, in the Danish West Indies, a colony consisting of three islands: St Thomas, St Jan and St Croix.

As always, Femi's clothes were changed to something more appropriate for the time period and location. 'Hmmm, a loose linen shirt and trousers. Considering the weather here, that makes sense.'

He found himself stranded on a beach. 'My missions seem to start on a beach or in a forest,' he noted. He was hungry and noticed some coconut palms close by the beach. He walked over to them and climbed up one to get himself some.

Whilst he was eating he suddenly heard a trigger clicking and felt a gun pressed against his cheek.

'What are you doing out here? Who gave you permission to come here and eat? Now get on your feet, slave. *Move* now!'

Femi decided to play along, and got up as instructed. But as he did so he grabbed some sand in his hands without his assailant noticing. After they had walked a few metres, Femi pretended to fall over.

Taking the bait, the man approached Femi: 'Get up! I didn't say you could take a break. We have to ...'

Femi was on the brink of making his move and attacking the man. But at the very last moment he changed his mind; he felt his mission would be best served in this case by going along with whatever was happening. He knew that his task here was to get on board the Fredensborg and free everyone on that ship, and stop it from reaching its destination, so he thought that his best bet would be to go wherever this man took him. So he dropped the sand and got back onto his feet.

'Don't you ever do that again. If you do, me and you are going to have some words. Now, let's go.' They walked to the other end of the beach, where the rest of the crew of the Fredensborg were waiting. They were in the process of rounding up slaves and preparing to board the ship.

'I've found a straggler, Captain.' The ship's captain was Espen Kiønigs. He had been hired by the ship owners. When he caught a glimpse of Femi he decided to take a closer look. He walked up to him and then around him, looking up and down at Femi, inspecting him as if he was a piece of furniture that he had acquired.

'Hmm, this one looks fresh,' Captain Kiønigs said sharply. 'What's your name, slave?'

Femi looked the captain in the eyes and didn't say a word.

Noting the silence the captain said, 'Either you're the silent type or you don't understand a word of English. But you look strong. I think I'll get a good price for you. Yo, Maurice, come over here and ask this guy what his name is.'

Another member of the crew came onto the scene. To Femi's surprise he wasn't Caucasian like the rest of the crew. He was black. If anything, his skin colour resembled the rest of the slaves that the captain had acquired. Maurice spoke in a local West Indies dialect, but Femi, not being of West Indian origin, did not understand a word of what Maurice was asking him and didn't respond.

'Very well,' said the captain. 'Have it your way. Just know this; your behind now belongs to me. Right, men, chain him up with the other cargo. We'll head out within the next ten minutes.

Femi was dragged over to the cargo that Captain Kiønigs was referring to. To Femi's surprise the cargo wasn't some material possession. It was slaves. Captain Kiønigs and his crew had come to the West Indies to gather slaves to leverage within the trade routes in Europe.

'*Move*, son.' But Femi, not budging, was kneed in his shins, and ended up falling to his knees on the beach.

His assailant chained him up with the other slaves. 'There we go. That's your position in this world; right below us. Welcome to your future; like the captain said, from now on you're *our* property.'

When they went away Femi tried to see if he could break out of his chains. He struggled and squirmed, but to no avail.

'Forget it, we've already tried. Unless you have the strength of a bear you ain't getting out of those chains.'

Femi looked up to see who had said these words. It turned out to be a man who was sitting, chained up, opposite to him.

'Thanks for the tip. But we have to do something to get out of here.'

'We can't. Even if by some miracle if we do manage to escape they'll come back and grab us again. That's how things work around here.'

'Interesting; what is your name?'

'Desmond Norris. What's yours, stranger?'

'I'm Femi Adebayo.'

'Well, Femi, nice to meet you. Judging by your accent I take it you're not from this island.'

'No, I live in London, but my roots are Nigerian. My tribe is the Yoruba.'

'Wait – did you say Yoruba?'

'Yes, Yoruba. Why?'

'The Yoruba warriors are amongst the most feared in the world. They're legendary! After staving off the threat of the Portuguese a few hundred years ago, they helped to grow the rest of Africa. Africa grew to be such a power that no one in America or Europe would even dare think of trying to invade them after that. That's why the rest of the world has been made to suffer. But if you're from there, what are you doing here? You'd be safe over there. Why come here?'

'I was sent here to help you,' Femi responded.

'Great! Some hope at last. How many others are here?'

'There's no one else, Desmond. I'm the only one.'

'Just you? With all due respect, Femi, you're just one man. Captain Espen Kiønigs has a crew. How are you going to take them all on?'

'I've taken on armies and beaten them before. Just give me time to formulate a plan. Until then we have to keep a low profile. And keep what I just told you to yourself. Understood?'

'Your secret's safe with me, Femi.'

'Ok, the captain and his crew are approaching us. Let's keep quiet and see what they have to say for themselves.'

Captain Kiønigs began to address the captives: 'Ladies and gentlemen, for those of you who don't know me, I am Captain Espen Kiønigs. You may address me as Captain. From this point on your behinds belong to me. You will eat when I say, you will work when I say, and you will do what I say. Failure to obey my commands or a drop in your capacity to carry them out and you'll be thrown overboard. No second chances. Now, we're all going to go on a little trip. We're going to set sail on that little beauty over there.'

Kiønigs pointed in the direction of the ship at anchor in the bay. It was a sight to behold, one of the more impressive slave ships of its time.

'Behold the Fredensborg,' he continued menacingly. 'This treasure is going to be your home for the next few weeks. We're going to be taking a trip to Copenhagen; and you, ladies and gentlemen, are the cargo. You're going to make me rich. So if any of you try to mess around with me you mess around with my money. And, trust me, you won't like it if you mess around with my money. So it won't be good if any of you try to cross me. Is that understood?'

None of the captives dared to say anything. They were too intimidated by the captain's words.

'Right, let's get this show on the road. Men, load up the cargo. Time is money. We need to get sailing. Jack, a word please.'

Jack was the man who had found Femi.

'Yes, Captain.'

'I'm going to need a favour from you whilst we are at sea. The one you found. I need you to keep an eye on him. He has strength, and could be a problem.'

'He's just one man. What kind of trouble could he be?'

'It only takes one spark to light a fire. We have a lot of money riding on this. With this cargo we could live like kings for the rest of our lives. So any nonsense, let me know immediately. Does that make sense?'

'Any trouble and I'll let you know straight away,' Jack promised the captain.

'Excellent; that's excellent indeed. Now let's get aboard, set sail and claim our riches.'

'Aye, aye, Captain,' Jack responded, laughing at the captain's remarks.

Meanwhile the rest of the crew were busy getting all the captives onto the ship. A lot of them cried out in horror. For many of them, the West Indies was all they had ever known. Not only were they leaving behind their homeland; they were leaving behind their family and loved ones. The comfort of home was about to be replaced by a life of purgatory. The reality of this began to dawn on them when the crew prepared to set sail.

Finally Captain Kiønigs and Jack went on board the Fredensborg, and the captain said, 'It's time to go, men. Set sail, weigh anchor, and get this ship moving.' The Fredensborg left the shores of the West Indies and began its long voyage to Copenhagen.

As the ship moved further and further away from the shores of the West Indies, Desmond took one final glance at the shores in the sad belief that this was a one-way trip.

Femi observing the glance at the shore, reached out to him to try to reassure him: 'Desmond, are you all right?'

'No I'm not all right. We in the West Indies don't have much. But for as long as I can remember I've always been able to walk out onto the beach and be blessed by the sun. But now that very simple privilege has been taken away from me. What have I done to deserve this? In fact, what have any of us done?'

'Stay strong, Desmond. We'll get back here, I promise you. Just hang in there.'

Chapter 20: Witness the pain of the Fredensborg

The Fredensborg had been sailing across the high seas for a couple of days. The conditions of the ship were not suitable for the number of passengers it was carrying. The slaves found themselves sleeping in the lower decks of the ship with very little headroom.

To help get through the weary days, the slaves would often sing songs to themselves to keep their spirits high. One song the women could often be heard singing was 'Linstead Market', a song passed on to them from their cousins in Jamaica:

Mi carry mi ackee go a Linstead Market
Not a quattie worth sell.
Mi Carry me ackee go a Linstead Market'
Not a quattie worth sell.
Lord what night, not a bite
What a Saturday night
Lawd what a night not a bite
What a Saturday night.
Everybody come feel up, feel up

The Mission to End Slavery

Not a quattie worth sell,
Everybody come feel up, feel up
Not a quattie worth sell.

Lord what night, not a bite
What a Saturday night,
Lawd what a night not a bite
What a Saturday night.
Do mi mommy nuh beat mi kill mi
Sake a Merry-go-round,
Do mi mommy don't beat me kill mi
Sake a American rum.
Lord what night, not a bite
What a Saturday night,
Lawd what a night not a bite
What a Saturday night.

All di pickney dem a linga linga
Fi weh dem mumma no bring,
All di pickney dem a linga linga
Fi weh dem mumma no bring.
Lawd, what a night, not a bite
What a Satiday night,
Lawd, what a night, not a bite
How di pickney gwine feed?'

Once when they were singing this song the captain came down with his crew to see what the noise was about.

'What on earth are you people singing?'

'What's the matter, Captain, you don't like singing?' one of the captives asked.

'That isn't singing. That's noise. I hate noise, as it stops me thinking. And when I can't think I can't make plans. No plans no money. You get it. So cut out the noise,' the captain demanded.

'What is this? You take us away from our homelands. You feed us scraps. You make us sleep in this hellhole. Haven't we suffered enough?'

Captain Kiønigs in retaliation struck the captive in the face: 'Suffering, you call this suffering? You don't know the meaning of the word. However, if you're so keen to experience true suffering, that I can easily arrange for you. Guards bring out the whip.' One of the crew brought out the terrible multi-strand whip for him. Captain Kiønigs was not going to let this incident go unpunished.

'Twenty lashes.'

The guards strapped the captive to a grating and whipped him in front of everyone.

The man yelled for mercy. 'Please, no more! I'm sorry! Ahhh ...' He screamed in agony, but to no avail, and passed out.

Many of the other captives saw this mistreatment at first hand. They were shocked to see such cruelty, and were horrified at the lengths the captain would go to. It was clear that Captain Espen Kiønigs, not content with taking their freedom of body, also wanted to take their freedom of mind. He had let everyone know that he was in charge, and had no qualms about the way he would achieve his goals.

'That, everyone, is a lesson in what happens when you step out of line. If you ever feel like disobeying my orders, remember what you've just witnessed. This is your last warning.'

The captain headed back up to the main deck with his senior officers.

As he walked by, Femi gave him a stern look. 'Someday you're going to get yours, you bastard,' Femi thought to himself as he growled silently in impotent anger.

As time went on things got worse and worse for the captives on the ship. Eventually some of them started to fall victim to scurvy. The crew noticed this and reported it to the captain, who went down to the lower deck to find out what was going on.

'Some of the captives are sick.'

'How many?' the captain asked.

'Only four of them at the moment.'

'We'll need to see if they're any good for work. Check if any of them can still stand.'

But all four of them were unable to get to their feet.

'Hmmm, damaged goods,' said the captain. 'I can't sell sick people. I have no use for them. They could also pass on whatever disease they have to the other slaves. Throw 'em overboard.'

The guards took the four sick captives and dragged them to the upper deck.

'No, please, my baby,' screamed one woman.

'No, I beg you!' screamed another. The captives were stunned, disbelieving, horrified at the captain's disregard for human life in the name of profit. Among the sick people was a young girl aged barely eight, and the others were two men in their twenties and a woman.

The captain had sentenced a child, two husbands and a wife to die. He simply looked on as one by one they were thrown overboard and left to drown.

Heading back down to the lower deck, the captain looked at the slaves. They were in tears, in despair at seeing their loved ones die – all because someone had decided their life had no more meaning.

'Like I said to you when you got here, you're all my property. If you stop being useful to me I'll throw you out to the sharks. Stay healthy you live; if you become sick you die. It's that simple.'

Femi had seen enough and finally decided to say something. 'You're despicable. I've seen some really cruel men, but you're by far the worst. You're a not a businessman. You're a murderer, a cold-blooded killer.'

Captain Espen Kiønigs lowered his gaze to Femi. 'Ah, so he *does* speak. Bosun, get this man onto his feet.'

The captain then walked over to Femi. Staring him directly in the eyes, the captain said, 'I can see you have inner strength. You could be useful. I have some manual labour tasks that could do with a man of your abilities. You're more useful than those diseased people now at the bottom of the sea.'

Enraged, Femi head-butted the captain, knocking him down to the deck. The guards grabbed him. The captain staggered back onto his feet, reached for his gun and aimed it at Femi at point-blank range.

The captain wanted to make an example of Femi – but then his greedy self wouldn't allow him to do so; smirking, the captain put his gun away, saying, 'Never make a decision when you're angry. It leads to bad business decisions. Boy, this is your lucky day. I'm not going to kill you – you're more valuable to me alive than dead. Consider this an extension of my generosity.' The captain thumped Femi in the stomach, bringing him to his knees.

Then he said, 'C'mon boys, back to the upper deck. The message is clear.'

The slaves were left to reflect on the events that had taken place that day. As night fell, morale amongst the captives dropped lower than ever. Desmond especially was worried for his people.

'Are you all right Femi?'

'I'm fine, Desmond. The captain will need to hit me harder than that to keep me down.'

'You need to be careful. He's a psychopath. He could easily have chosen to end your life today. Without you, we don't stand a chance in hell. Tread carefully, Femi.'

'I just had to say something. He needs to know that we can't be bullied. We can't let him break us.'

'I'm not sure how much more of this we can take. I mean, look at this. Look at how we're sleeping. Dogs have better living conditions than this. We're getting treated like cattle here. The captain doesn't see us as human beings at all.'

'Just hang tight, Desmond. I may have found a way to beat him.'

'Really? How? Do tell me.'

One of the crew came down to the lower deck. 'Right, everyone, enough chatter. You all need to go to sleep now. Your noise is disturbing the captain.' Everyone began to settle down for the night.

Femi whispered, 'We'll finish this in the morning, Desmond.'

'Very well, then. Sleep well, Femi.'

After a while the sailor on guard went back to the upper deck to get some air, assuming that everyone was asleep. But Femi was still wide awake, unable to sleep after the whipping and the murders.

'Not a pretty sight, is it, Femi?'

Femi could recognise that voice from anywhere: 'Mr Diggity, the one and only!'

'Hey, warrior. How you holding up?'

'To be honest with you, I'm feeling lousy. Today what I witnessed was beyond words. It was vulgar. It was vile. People are dying on this ship. We're crammed into this small space like cattle, we're barely getting enough food. Disease is beginning to run rampant here. Anyone they deem not useful they simply toss over and send them to an early grave deep within the ocean. If this continues, hardly anyone's going to make it.'

'Very early on in this mission I said to you, *how can you fix the problem if you don't know what the problem is in the first place?*'

'You did, Mr Diggity, you did indeed. I thought what I saw in West Virginia was bad. But the treatment we're getting here is way worse. I need to find a solution, and fast.'

'So what's your play? Have any ideas crept into your head yet?' Mr Diggity asked intently.

'I need to get some of the crew on my side; the ones that come from the West Indies. They're slaves, too. They're here by force. They act as intermediaries between us and the permanent crew.'

'Slave ships like this one often used locals for that purpose. They did this partly to help overcome any language barriers, but also to try to keep the slaves at ease by seeing people of their own culture. So what you're telling me comes as no surprise. Although it doesn't appear to be working here, for the obvious reason.'

'That's precisely my point, Mr Diggity. They don't want to be here an more than the rest of us. I can see it in their eyes when they are carrying out tasks such as throwing the sick people overboard this morning. If I can convince them, they'll help.'

'I see you're putting what you learned in West Virginia to good use, Femi.'

'It's like that saying in my own time Mr Diggity: those who don't learn from their past are doomed to repeat it. There's only one thing I haven't figured out yet.'

'Really? What's that?'

'Why did the time computer state that I needed to come here? I mean there are more famous slave ships, such as the Clotilda. What's so special about this one?'

'To answer that, you need to look at where this ship's been going,' Mr Diggity said.

'All right, then; well, based on what I've learned during my time here, this ship travels around the Caribbean then goes back and forth to Europe. Wait a minute … that's it, isn't it? Because the triangular trade never started after all, the transatlantic route to Europe is now one of the key slave trading routes. If we are able to disrupt this flow of slaves it will help prevent transatlantic slavery from ever being possible as well.'

'Bingo! That's precisely why computer picked those missions. To change the course of history you can't just go anywhere. As with a length of rope, you have to cut it in the right spots to completely break the chain. Stopping this ship from reaching the Danish shores will have a knock-on effect that will bring in the necessary changes. It sounds as if you know what you need to do. Just hang in there. I must go – the guard's coming back. Good luck.'

'Thanks; I'm going to need it.'

Mr Diggity disappeared just as the guard re-entered the lower deck and shouted: 'You there! Stop making noise and get back to sleep.'

'Yes *sir*,' Femi sarcastically replied. As he went to sleep he pondered how to get the West Indian trusties to revolt with him and help him rescue the slaves on the ship.

Chapter 21: Taking over the Fredensborg

At dawn the next day Femi began plotting the downfall of Captain Espen Kiønigs. Femi knew that with his hands and feet literally tied he couldn't go on the attack in the manner he was accustomed to.

So he started to observe the crew. He spotted that they were working on a rota. Maurice in particular seemed to be the one that watched over them at night and during the middle of the day. Femi had made up his mind to persuade Maurice to turn against the captain.

During one of Maurice's midday shifts he was dishing out rations to the slaves. After doing his normal rounds he approached Femi. Femi spilled some of his ration.

'What are you doing? You're lucky I don't have you whipped for that!' As Maurice crouched down to clean up the mess, Femi whispered in his ear, 'When you're on your night shift come and find me. We need to talk.'

Maurice carried on, pretending not to have heard what Femi had said to him. He completed handing out the rations and headed back to the upper deck.

Desmond asked Femi, 'Did he hear your message?'

'He heard me all right. Whether he decides to act upon it is another matter.'

Night time came. Femi waited for Maurice to come. He waited and waited. Eventually he gave up and fell asleep. But later on he felt a tap on his shoulder.

'You asked to speak with me. So here I am.'

'Great,' Femi, bleary-eyed, responded.

'It's time we talked.'

'Tell me, Maurice. Look around you. What do you see?'

Maurice took a glance round. 'I see a slave ship.'

Disconcerted, Femi replied, 'Really? Is that all? Look again.'

Again Maurice looked round the ship: 'Ok, I see the slaves.'

'Is that really all you see, Maurice? Let me tell you what I see. I see a group of innocent people who've been mistreated and starved, and beaten and whipped whenever they stand up for themselves. I see a group of people who've been taken away from their homes against their own free will, whose basic human rights have been trampled on. And I'm standing in front of an Uncle flipping Tom who's so blind to this filth and has his head so far up his arse he betrays his own people.'

'How *dare* you? You know nothing about me!' Maurice reacted furiously to Femi's comments.

'What, the truth hurts doesn't it? Wake up; we're being treated like dogs down here. And you sit there and carry out Captain Espen Kiønigs' every command. Tell me how you felt when you saw those sick people being thrown overboard, Maurice. What if it was one of your loved ones that were killed like that just because they were deemed to no longer be of service?'

'I don't have a choice.'

'Yes you do, Maurice.'

'We're stuck here. There's no way out of this.'

'There's always a way. Sometimes the answer's staring you in the face.'

Maurice paused for a moment. Suddenly curious, he wished to learn more: 'So, what are you proposing?'

'It's simple rebellion.'

'What?'

'You heard me, Maurice, rebellion. You're close to the captain. You can help us get rid of these chains; you can help us fight back. We can win our freedom.'

'I can't, Femi. If the captain found out he'd kill me.'

'What you rather have? A long life where you have no choice and are just someone else's lapdog? Or a life of freedom, where you get to decide your own destiny?'

'We wouldn't succeed.'

'We have to try or we're already dead.'

'I'm sorry, I can't do this. We'll soon be in Denmark. Just hang on till then. I have to go. My relief will take over shortly.'

Femi looked on in disgust as Maurice walked away. Femi could not comprehend why Maurice would not want to help.

But Maurice could not forget Femi's words. They haunted him throughout the next day. Maurice had met Captain Espen Kiønigs some years prior to this voyage, and the captain had promised Maurice a better life for him and his family. Now, upon reflection Maurice wondered whether he had done the right thing. He had more money now, but his homeland was in a worse state than ever, so his family weren't happy.

In the afternoon whilst Maurice was on duty the captain came down to the lower deck. He was in a joyous mood and had a devilish smile on his face: 'Today I'm in the mood for some entertainment. I need something fresh and exotic. Let's see what we have here.'

The captain started inspecting the females amongst the slaves, and a girl who was barely sixteen caught his eye.

'Hmmm, you'll do. Bosun, unchain this one and bring her to my cabin.'

Bosun did exactly that despite her screams. About an hour later he returned the girl and chained her up again. She wept bitterly.

'My dear, what happened? What did the captain do to you?' Desmond asked.

'He ... raped me.' A deafening silence surrounded the room, a silence that rapidly turned into disgust and anger. This was the final straw.

Maurice's mind was now made up. That night when Femi was asleep, he felt a tap on his shoulder. When he awoke Maurice was standing before him.

'Enough of this crap. Captain Espen Kiønigs has to be stopped. If we don't do something now we'll never be free. So this rebellion idea of yours; where do we begin?'

Femi smiled at Maurice's change of heart. 'All right, then. Let's talk business.'

Femi and Maurice spent the next few nights plotting how they were going to make the rebellion work. Their plan was to strike just before dawn. Maurice's task was to steal the keys to the chains. He would then help the slaves get the weapons that would enable them to take over the ship. To ensure that their plan was kept a secret, only Desmond would be made aware of what was going on. It was agreed that they would strike the next morning.

Just before dawn, Maurice woke up, looked around and saw that most of the crew were still asleep. Silently he made his way to the captain's cabin; the keys were kept in the pocket of the captain's coat, which he hung just inside the door. Very gently and cautiously Maurice opened the door, reached into the pocket and filched the keys.

He made his way to the lower deck, where the slaves were kept. The crewman guarding them was fast asleep. Maurice promptly woke him up.

'Get up! The captain needs us. Let's go.'

'Sure, Maurice, you lead the way.'

'No – after you. I insist.'

The guard had taken just a couple of steps when Maurice grabbed him from behind, covering his mouth, and stabbed him in the back. Femi and the other slaves began to awaken and saw what Maurice had done. Maurice freed Femi first.

'Quickly, free the others! The crew will soon awaken.'

Once the slaves were free from their chains Maurice led them to a room where the weapons were stored: 'Each of you grab a weapon and prepare yourselves. If you want your freedom you'll have to fight for it.'

Femi spotted a sword in the corner of the room. He went over and picked it up. He instinctively began practising his sword fighting drills. Everyone was taken aback by the skill Femi showcased.

'I have everything I need right here,' he remarked.

The slaves charged out of the weapons room and started attacking the crew. The slaves were keen to make sure that the crew experienced the same torture and pain that they had been subjected to.

Femi's and Maurice's plan was going exactly as they had planned. The slaves began to overrun the ship and had the crew cowering in fear. The noise woke the captain up, as one of the crew ran into his cabin.

'Captain, the slaves have been freed. They're rebelling and have begun to take over the ship.'

'How did they get free? The keys are …' The captain ran over to his coat and searched for the keys. Upon realising that they had vanished he vowed, 'Whoever did this will *pay!*'

He ordered his crew to take back control of the ship. The slaves had the greater numbers, but the captain's gun was a great equaliser.

'Like I said to you all at the beginning, you do something I don't like there'll be consequences,' he said as he started shooting slaves.

During the confrontation the captain spotted Maurice helping the slaves to attack his crew.

'MAURICE!' Captain Espen Kiønigs yelled in fury. 'How *dare* you? It was you who stole the keys. I took you from the bush and made you into a wealthy man, and this is how you repay me.'

'You didn't do me any favours. You made me into another slave. I won't betray my people any more. Now I'm free.'

'Oh, so you want your freedom? Hmmm. Here's your fucking freedom!' The captain shot Maurice in the head and smirked as Maurice's lifeless body dropped to the deck.

Femi witnessed Maurice's brutal execution. In retaliation he took apart four members of the crew. After making his way through the melée the captain came face to face with Femi, raised his gun and pointed it at him.

'You; it was *you* who did this!' the captain screamed at Femi.

'No, *you* did this. I just lit the torch. When you bring people nothing but misery, torture and enslavement, they will always rise against up against you,' Femi replied.

'I should have killed you before,' said the captain, pulling the trigger. But unfortunately for Espen he fired it to no avail. He had run out of bullets.

'Huh! What are you going to do now?'

'I don't need a gun to kill you. I'll finish you off with this.' The captain drew his sword and Femi raised his, ready to battle the captain. The captain charged at Femi and swung his sword ferociously at Femi. Femi's training with Chief Oko in the art of swordplay was still ingrained in him. He easily avoided the captain's wild swings and elegantly and calmly timed his attacks. As the fight went on Captain Espen Kiønigs grew more irritated and more erratic.

At one point both men's swords clashed above their heads. Seizing the moment Femi head-butted the captain, then punched him in the face for good measure, making him fall to the ground.

As he struggled to get up, Captain Espen Kiønigs looked up and saw Femi in good form; he had already resumed his battle stance, ready to continue the fight. The captain was taken aback by Femi's swordsmanship.

'I have to admit you've surprised me, Femi. For a slave your skill is exceptional. It's a shame I have to kill you. You would've made a fine fighter as a member of my crew.'

'I would never fight for a man like you. I'm here to stop men like you. It's what the Yoruba warriors trained me to do. Now let's end this.'

'Yoruba warriors? No wonder you can fight. I'll kill you to teach them to stay out of my affairs.'

The fight resumed. Enraged, the captain became yet more erratic, and Femi eventually knocked the captain's sword out of his hand. Femi gave Captain Espen Kiønigs a beating. Eventually the captain found himself lying on his back against the binnacle. He was faced with nothing but the tip of Femi's sword.

The captain was at Femi's mercy; Femi could end his life whenever he wanted.

'What are you waiting for? Get this over with. At least give me an honourable death. *DO IT!!!!!*'

'No, Captain. It isn't going to be that easy for you. You don't get the easy release of death. You're going to live. And you're going to suffer. We're going to make your life hell. You're going to live, and you're going to experience what we've had to go through over the decades. You're going to know what it's like to be treated like an animal. After you have suffered the lowest of lows, then and only then will you have my permission to die.'

Captain Espen Kiønigs and his crew had been beaten. The ship had been taken over and the slaves were free. The slaves looked at Femi in admiration as he proclaimed: 'Freedom! You are slaves no longer. The days of you all having to lead this life are over. Captain Espen Kiønigs can harm you no longer. This man is now your prisoner. You can do with him what you wish.'

Desmond, speaking on behalf of his people, said, 'Femi, we're forever in your gratitude for helping to set us free. We only have one simple request. We want to go home. We want to return to our families and our own way of life.'

'No problem. Captain, your first task will be to navigate these people back to the home you stole them from. So come on, get to work.'

The slaves spent the next few weeks sailing the Fredensborg back to the Danish West Indies where this journey had begun, reluctantly guided by the captain, and using the position of the sun and stars to check where they were going to ensure that he was telling them the truth. Upon arrival on the shores of St Thomas, a mixture of emotions was experienced by the slaves. On one hand there was relief that the pain that they had felt and witnessed on the Fredensborg had come to an end. On the other was happiness and pure joy at seeing their homeland again and being reunited with the people they thought they had left behind forever.

Femi and Desmond Norris disembarked.

'So we're back in the spot where we first met each other,' Desmond said.

Femi smiled at Desmond and said, 'Indeed we are. Indeed we are. The question is now we're back what's the plan? I mean, what now?'

'For now, we enjoy being back and we catch up on what we missed. It's been a while,' Desmond suggested.

'Something still needs to be done about that infamous captain over there.'

'I think we can find a use for him, Femi. He is, at the end of a day, a soldier. Our borders will need defending. As despicable as he is, he can maybe show us how we can defend ourselves and help prevent this from ever happening again, That's the least he can do for all the harm he has caused us; then he can rot in prison for his crimes. Perhaps we can also use this to free ourselves from the Danish. It's about time we stood on our own feet. Our reliance on outsiders created this mess.'

'Sounds like a plan, Desmond.'

'What are you going to do, Femi? Will you return to your homeland?'

'Not just yet. I have one more stop that I need to make before I go home. After that, my mission's done. So for now I bid you farewell, Desmond. I was lucky to have met you.'

'The pleasure was all mine.'

Desmond and Femi embraced each other for the final time before Femi departed.

'Goodbye, my friend. I'll be seeing you.'

Femi walked back down the beach. He came across the coconut palm he had climbed when he had arrived in the Danish West Indies. Remembering that he had never got to finish his coconut that time, he got another one and whilst eating it reflected on the adventure he had just had.

Femi had been on this mission now for considerably more than a year. He began to reflect on what he had had to overcome, the people that he had met and the changes he had been able to make. He also began to think about how he had grown as a person. Looking back to his first encounter with Mr Diggity, he had lost a lot of assumptions that he had made about slavery. The issue in certain areas wasn't as clear-cut as he had first thought.

When Femi had finished his coconut he got up and prepared to face his final mission.

'It's time to take down the Romans. *It's time to resume the mission.*' The time bracelet reappeared with the last bead glowing. As Femi tapped it, the time door appeared. The final encounter awaited him. Some interesting surprises were waiting for him, too, as he was about to face arguably his most dangerous opponent; the mighty and legendary Roman Empire.

Chapter 22: Meeting Queen Amanirenas

Femi was transported to his final destination. As usual, upon arrival his clothing changed into something more appropriate and his bracelet disappeared. He took a moment to reflect on his new attire.

'Nifty! Now to find this Queen Amanirenas.

He walked for a few miles, eventually coming across a small town. It was densely populated; everyone was busy with their daily routine. In an attempt to get some intel he decided to approach one of the locals.

'Excuse me, there.'

'What can I do for you, stranger?'

'This is the Kush Kingdom, correct?'

'Correction; it is the Great Kush Kingdom.'

'Good, I'm in the right place. I'm looking for someone.'

'Everyone's looking for someone here, stranger.'

'I'm looking for Queen Amanirenas.'

'Queen Amanirenas, huh! Everyone is always trying to get with Queen Amanirenas. I can understand why. She's as beautiful as the River Nile itself. Rest assured, though, she's as tough as she's beautiful. If she doesn't like you she'll have your head cut off instantly and fed to the lions.'

'That's reassuring,' Femi responded, slightly startled by this statement. 'Where would I be able to find her?'

'Why, in her palace of course. You see that divine set of buildings over there? That's her palace. It's heavily guarded, though. No one gets in without the consent of the Queen.'

'Interesting; this just got a little bit more complicated.'

'What's your interest in the Queen? You don't seem to be interested in getting with her.'

'I need her help to take down the Romans.'

'Ah, those son of the bitches. I can't stand them! They think they can walk all over us and add our people to their list of slaves. We showed them, though.'

'Wait – the Romans have attacked here previously?'

'Yep, but we beat them and forced them to fall back. Our victory came at a cost, though. A lot of good men and women lost their lives during that battle.'

Femi found this information very good; it was in line with what Mr Diggity had told him about the Kush Kingdom. It also clarified in his own mind why the Egyptians would be needed to succeed in this mission.

'This is why I'm here. I'm here to stop the Romans once and for all.'

'Ha! – you really think you can stop the Romans?'

Defiantly, Femi responded, 'Yes, I can.'

'You're really serious, aren't you?'

Femi nodded his head.

'What's your name, stranger?'

'I'm called Femi.'

'Well then, Femi, I'm Mido. You're either a brave man or a damn fool. But if you're really serious about getting to meet the Queen, you're going to have to sneak in. Right now it's the middle of day and you would be spotted easily and be killed. Your best bet is sneaking in at sunset. I think I can help you get in; but only on one condition. If he's still alive, free my brother.'

'Your brother?'

'Yes, Femi; my brother, Karim. He was taken prisoner when the Romans came here before. I miss him and I'd do anything to get him back. But no one is prepared to go to Rome and rescue him. Find out what happened to him, and if he's alive bring him back home.'

'You have my word, Mido; I'll find your brother and if he's alive I'll rescue him.'

'All right, warrior, we have a deal. Right now, here's how you can get into the palace.'

Hours passed until sunset came to the Kush Kingdom. At sunset the guards routinely picked up a new set of barrels of beverages for the palace, and took them into the palace kitchen. It was Mido's shop that provided the beverages, and he hid Femi in one of the barrels.

As soon as Femi was inside the palace kitchen and heard no more movement, he opened the lid and got out of the barrel. Making his way out of the kitchen he started to sneak around in an attempt to find the Queen.

He managed to avoid the guards. Eventually he came across a meeting room where he heard something akin to a debate going on. He hid behind the door and listened in to see if he could get a clue as to where the Queen was. He was in luck, as behind the door she was speaking with her generals and advisors about how best to deal with the Romans.

'My Queen,' said her best general, Aton, 'the Romans are scared of us. We should advance. We should take them down now. I guarantee that they'll return. Caesar won't take their last defeat well.'

'General Aton, I understand your concern,' she said. 'I have no doubt that the Romans will return but I don't want to risk another bloodbath. A lot of my people died last time. We *will* attack them – but only when the time is right for us. We simply need to find a window of opportunity.'

Queen Amanirenas continued to debate the matter with her council.

But Femi had been spotted. 'You there, hold!' Two soldiers approached him, pointing their swords at his chest. Who are you? How did you get into the palace? What are you doing here?'

Femi held both his hands up to show surrender. 'Forgive the intrusion. I've come to see the Queen. I have a gift for her.'

'Gift? What gift?' asked one of the soldiers.

'Allow me to show you.' This diversion gave Femi the split second he needed to take out both the guards, with jab punches to their faces and roundhouse kicks to knock them unconscious. But one of the soldiers crashed into a statue in the hallway, creating a disturbance.

'What's that noise?' the queen shouted. More soldiers rushed in to check on the scene. General Aton and his advisers came out of the room.

'Seize him!' General Aton ordered.

Femi made a run for it. Numerous soldiers came at him and although he disarmed every single one of them, he found himself being chased all over the palace, avoiding soldiers at every turn.

Eventually he ran into the main palace hallway. Here his luck ran out. He found himself surrounded and had nowhere else to run.

'Surrender or die!' shouted General Aton.

'Hold on, General Aton,' said Queen Amanirenas. 'I want to see who our intruder is.' She walked between the soldiers to stand before Femi. He was taken aback at how beautiful she was, and in awe of how she took command of the situation so swiftly.

'You really are as beautiful as they say you are.'

Queen Amanirenas snapped, 'How *dare* you?'

'I'm sorry – a very poor choice of words.'

'How did you get in here?' she asked Femi.

'I sneaked inside via one of the barrels containing your drinks.'

'Hmm, Mido! I'll have his head for this.'

'Please forgive Mido. He only wanted to help me get justice against the Romans.' Her soldiers were beginning to move in on Femi. Queen Amanirenas held out her hand to make them back off. Keen to learn more, she said 'Justice against the Romans?'

Femi walked nearer her: 'Queen Amanirenas, please excuse my deception. I needed a way to get close to you. Please accept my humble apologies.' Femi bowed before the Queen. But she was not amused by his antics.

'How dare you? You come in here and disturb our proceedings, you attack my royal guards, and now you expect me to accept your apologies. Give me one reason why I shouldn't have you executed here and now.'

'I can help you.'

Queen Amanirenas laughed at Femi's response: 'Help me? How can *you* help me?'

'I can help you stop the Roman Empire. You know, Julius Caesar isn't a threat just to your people but a threat to people all over the world. The Kush Kingdom is strong, but to defeat the Roman Empire you'll need allies, my Queen. I am on a mission of a higher purpose, but to succeed I'm going to need your help. We're going to need each other.'

Queen Amanirenas reflected on Femi's words. 'Give me one reason why I should trust you.'

'Simple, because I trust you. I place my life in your hands.' Femi got down on one knee and offered Queen Amanirenas his sword. She accepted it.

'You have the option to end my life if you choose. But if you spare me I promise you that you'll not regret it.' Queen Amanirenas placed the sword on Femi's neck; she was in a position to strike. Femi started to wonder if his gamble was a big mistake. Had he come so far on his quest only to fail at the last hurdle? But she lowered the sword.

'Hmmm, I could have killed you, stranger. Why would you take this risk?'

Femi responded, 'It was the only way I could think of to show you I'm worthy of your trust.'

'What's your name, stranger?'

'My name's Femi Adebayo'

'Well, Femi Adebayo, welcome to the Kush Kingdom. I'm Queen Amanirenas. Follow me, Femi; I think we have much to discuss. Guards, follow us.'

The Queen took Femi on a tour of her palace. He noted how beautiful it was. She took him outside to observe the rest of their surroundings, and they were equally pleasant. Femi also saw something that surprised him. Pyramids. He hadn't been expecting to see them in the Kush Kingdom.

'Magnificent, aren't they, Femi?'

'Yes they are, Queen Amanirenas. But I thought pyramids existed in Egypt alone.'

'*Please*. Who do you think taught them how to build pyramids?'

'Really. How did you build them? I mean, they're so high. How did your builders get up there?'

'Well it's really quite simple, Femi. Using sledges, and wetting the sand to a certain degree made it easier to climb,' Queen Amanirenas responded.

'Well at least that mystery's cleared up,' Femi observed.

'You spoke of a higher purpose, Femi. So tell me, what brings you to my kingdom?'

Femi smiled. 'I'm on a mission to end slavery. I've travelled the world. I've been to West Africa. I've been to America and I've sailed across the high seas. I'm on the final part of my mission.'

'That's quite a few places,' said the Queen.

'My mission's taken me to places I never thought I'd ever go to; physically and mentally. Getting this far has taken every ounce of blood and sweat that I have.'

'Slavery is a disease that plagues this world, Femi. It has caused endless wars and has cost countless lives. I protected my people from it as long as I could. I too have had to do things that I never thought I'd never do. During these battles I lost many brothers and sisters.'

Femi remorseful said, 'I'm sorry to hear this.'

'Thank you, Femi. When I saw members of my people dying from this, I promised them all that I would continue the fight. The questions I have for you right now are these: What made you come here to the Kush Kingdom? And how can we help you with your noble cause?'

'Legend has it that the Kush Kingdom will stand up against the Roman Empire, and it is one of the few civilisations to go up against the Roman Empire and not be conquered. Your people are the key. I don't understand the full picture, but my sources indicate that the root of slavery lies within the Roman Empire. If we stop the Roman Empire, that will help put an end to slavery. It'll help wipe slavery out from the western world forever.'

'These sources that you have; what are they, and how reliable are they? What if the Roman Empire can't be destroyed? Even if we succeeded in destroying the Roman Empire there's still no guarantee that slavery will cease to exist.'

Femi was not in a position to reveal that he was from the future; she would never believe that.

'Queen Amanirenas, I understand why you have these questions, and what I'm asking of you is a lot to take in. Let's just say I have had a vision from the heavens. For now, all I can ask is that you trust in me.'

'Very well Femi; for now you have my trust. If you do anything that violates that trust, know that I will have your head.'

Femi was a little disturbed by this admission. Nevertheless he responded, 'Fair enough.'

'Ok, Mr Visionary, so how do we take down the Roman Empire?' she asked.

'We need to get help from the Egyptians. They have reason to hate the Roman Empire as well. We need to get Cleopatra's aid. There is only one stumbling block. Mark Antony.'

'Mark Antony – Caesar's right-hand man?' Queen Amanirenas said in shock.

'Yes, Mark Antony,' Femi said sharply. 'But from what I know, he's on good terms with Cleopatra. That's an obstacle we'll need to overcome. If Mark Antony were to alert the Romans to our plans everything would be in ruins.'

Queen Amanirenas nodded in agreement. 'We're on good terms with the Egyptians. We'll go to them and seek out an alliance. Be warned, though, slavery is rampant in their culture. They may not like your abolish-slavery-at-all-costs approach.'

Femi reflected on her comments. Everywhere he had been, the communities he had helped had wanted to get rid of slavery and so were only too eager to help him. This would be the first time on his journey that he would be visiting a non-white community that wouldn't want to see slavery abolished. It certainly wasn't something that Mr Diggity had warned him about. Femi wanted to understand more about this.

'Why do you say this, Queen Amanirenas?'

'Femi, like you I think slavery is wrong. I've seen up close what it can do to people. To be forced from your home, not having the freedom to live the life that you want to live, and being beaten – and the women being raped by the owners so that they can get more slaves for free. This I know.

'However, there are some parts of the world that have built their civilisations up on slavery. Slavery is seen as a way of life. Egypt is one of those places. Before we ask the Egyptians to join us in the fight against the Roman Empire, we're going to need to ask them to change their way of life. Otherwise, how could we expect them to fight against a system that they follow themselves?'

'Hmmm, Queen Amanirenas, you're as wise as you're beautiful.'

'Femi, are you trying to make me blush?'

'Maybe,' responded Femi cheekily.

'I'm not used to being complimented.'

'Well, Queen Amanirenas, keep this up and you may need to get used to it.'

At that very moment an arrow hit one of the guards in the chest, killing him. Another arrow whirred past Queen Amanirenas.

'Take cover!' shouted Femi. The Queen hid behind Femi and her guards. Arrows started to rain down on them, and the Queen, Femi and the guards headed to some nearby trees for cover.

Femi, looking out between the trees, glimpsed the assassin on the palace roof. Femi decided that the best form of defence was attack.

'Queen Amanirenas, stay here by the trees. I'll get this guy. I need a spear, a sword and a shield.'

'Guards, give him what he needs!' Queen Amanirenas shouted.

One of the guards gave Femi his spear, sword and shield. As Femi went to take the sword the guard said, 'Be careful – he's hiding in the shadows. To counter darkness you need light. Bring him out into the open and take him down.'

'I understand. I know what I need to do,' responded Femi.

Femi thought back to the time he had spent training in West Africa, in particular running the gauntlet, and how he had been able to duck and weave through the strikes aimed at him whilst he was completing his final test to become a Yoruba warrior. After taking a deep breath, he let out a huge roar and leapt out of the trees in pursuit of the assassin.

On seeing Femi the assassin started firing arrows. Femi's shield blocked the arrows from hitting him. The assassin continued to shoot, only stopping when he had run out of arrows

Femi, now knowing that he had the assassin on the run, continued the pursuit. 'I can't let him get away,' he said to himself. 'There may be other assassins out here putting the Queen in danger, and I may be able to get information on how I can stop them.'

The assassin knew that he had no other option but to run, so he started to head back down the roof. As he was about to exit the roof, guards who had heard the noise entered the palace rooftop.

'STOP!' the guards shouted. The assassin fled back down to the edge of the roof. He threw a looped rope at a pole ahead of him, and catching the top of the pole with it, he swung down the pole in a manner that would have made Indiana Jones proud.

By the time the assassin hit the ground he saw a rampaging Femi closing in on him, and Femi aimed his spear at the assassin, which hit him in his back. Screaming in agony, he fell to the ground.

'I have him!' yelled Femi. The Queen and her guards joined Femi, and they confronted the assassin.

The pain of the spear in his back was too much for the assassin to bear. Reaching round with his right hand he managed to pull it out. He tried to crawl away until a foot trod heavily on his hand. Yelling in agony again, he looked up and saw Femi, who was angry enough by now to take his head off.

Femi grabbed the assassin by his neck, half-choking him, and began his interrogation: 'Who are you?'

The assassin didn't answer.

'Talk, or I'll cut you up limb by limb and feed you to the lions.' And he squeezed the man's neck harder, throttling him.

The assassin gasped, 'My … my name's Aelius.'

'Aelius, huh?' growled Femi. 'Why are you here?'

'I was sent here to take out the Queen.'

'Who sent you here?' asked the Queen.

'My emperor; Gaius Julius Caesar.'

Queen Amanirenas asked, 'Why?'

'Because you're a threat to the empire. The Roman Empire needs to grow. Empires must continue to expand or die. With you out of the way your kingdom would have been easy pickings.'

'How many other assassins are with you?' Femi asked, squeezing Aelius's neck even tighter.

'The others will be here soon enough to bring your end. After the great Games, Caesar's sending his armies to Egypt. Once he is done with Egypt he's coming here. There's nothing you can do about it. Soon you'll all be dead or enslaved. Maybe even both. Hail Caesar!'

'Hail my sword, bitch!' Femi grabbed his sword and rammed it straight into Aelius, gutting him Aelius fell to the ground and died.

Understandably, Queen Amanirenas was disturbed by Aelius's words.

One of the guards asked, 'My Queen, what shall we do?'

'I'll tell you what we're going to do,' said Femi. 'We're going to fight. Meeting Aelius was a blessing in disguise. Now we know what the Romans are planning.'

Queen Amanirenas said, 'Femi's right. We need to act now. The games last for 30 days. This is the window of opportunity we've been looking for. Guards! Send a squad to the border and take out any remaining Roman assassins you find. When you return, we'll leave for Egypt and convince them to join our course. Prepare our armies; we're going to take the fight to the Romans. We'll do this while they're distracted by the Games and strike them down when they're at their most vulnerable.'

'Yes, my Queen.' A section of the guards immediately left to go and find the other assassins.

'Until they return, what are we supposed to do?' asks Femi.

'I thank you for your bravery today, Femi; you've risked so much for someone you don't know.'

'It was no trouble at all, Queen Amanirenas.'

'Tonight you will be sleeping with me, Femi.'

'Excuse me?' said Femi, confused.

'I presume you have no place to stay, as you're not from around here,' she responded, with a wide smile on her face.

'That's true.'

'Tonight you'll join me for dinner in the palace. We have spare rooms. You can rest there.'

'I will be honoured, my Queen. I accept your offer.'

'Good. It's settled. Now come, let us go and eat. I believe this is going to be start of a great partnership.'

'So do I, my Queen, so do I.'

Chapter 23: Exploring the Kush Kingdom

Femi woke up at dawn. This had become second nature to him due to his time training in West Africa. He headed down to the palace courtyards and practised his drills. As always, he started off with the drills he had been taught whilst learning the art of hand-to-hand combat. Later on, he picked up his sword and started practising his swordplay.

Whilst Femi was practising Queen Amanirenas, an early riser herself, was wandering around the palace. She spotted him, then watched him practising from a distance. She was deeply impressed with what she was seeing. She knew that in Femi she was observing a complete fighter. Fast but powerful, he had skill and precision in equal measure, but he also had the heart and the courage needed to win battles.

'He's a great warrior, my Queen,' General Uh Faham said as he walked up the balcony to stand beside her.

She nodded in agreement. 'His fighting skill is truly exceptional for someone so young. I wonder who he was trained by. It's as if he has been fighting for years.'

'His footwork is somewhat similar to our own,' the general noted. 'I think his training has origins in Africa, but I haven't come across anyone that combines the finesse with a natural killer instinct like he does. Not even the Romans can fight like this.'

'We have found a very powerful ally in Femi, General Uh Faham. With him by our side we can finally end the threat of the Roman Empire once and for all. As long as Caesar's alive this world will never know peace.'

'Be very careful, my Queen. We don't know anything about this Femi.'

'This man is not our enemy. I could have killed him the moment he got here. Then he risked his own life to save me. He's earned our gratitude as well as my trust.'

'Hmmm, that may be so. He was able to hold his own against a squad of our best men. That's impressive. But that skill could also be a danger to us if it turns out he's against us.'

'You worry too much,' the Queen said.

'It's my worrying that helps safeguard the kingdom. It's also why you put me in charge of your army.'

Queen Amanirenas smiled. 'That's true, General. But Femi is a good man. Wherever he's from, we can trust him.'

'If only we knew more about him. I always like to know who I'm going into battle with.'

'All right, General, I'll ask him.' Queen Amanirenas promptly walked off, heading down to the palace courtyard to join Femi.

Femi, still practising, continued with his swordplay. He didn't noticed that Queen Amanirenas had entered the courtyard. She kept quiet. Even so, she had hoped that Femi would notice her. But realising that she couldn't get Femi's attention due to his focus and intensity on his training, she decided to try a different tactic.

'Hmm not bad,' she called.

Femi stopped and turned round to see her. 'Queen Amanirenas, my apologies; I didn't notice you there.'

'No worries; I could tell you were deep in your training. Tell me, Femi, do you do this every morning?'

'Pretty much. I need to stay sharp. The day I'm not sharp is the day my mission fails.'

'Your training; it's impressive. Who were you taught by? You move in a manner that not even the Romans can match.'

'I was trained by the Yoruba tribe of West Africa,' Femi replied.

'Who are they? I have never heard of the Yoruba.'

'You will. Just give it time.'

'Time eh? So Mr Warrior, do you ever take a break?'

Taken aback slightly, Femi asked, 'How do you mean?'

'Follow me: you haven't been shown around the Kush Kingdom yet.'

'Sure. Lead the way, O Queen.'

As Femi and Queen Amanirenas were exiting the courtyard General Uh Faham came to join them.

'General Faham!'

'Yes, my Queen.'

'I am going to taking Femi for a tour of the Kush Kingdom. I think it's time he saw the sights.'

'My Queen, forgive my intrusion but do you think that's wise? You were almost killed yesterday.'

'I appreciate your concern, General.'

'But what if there are more assassins out there?'

'Then I will have my guardian warrior, Femi, to protect me. Prepare the troops! Once the remaining assassins have been disposed of, we'll head to Egypt immediately.'

'Yes, my Queen.'

Femi and the Queen continued on their way. Eventually they came across a stable of horses. The queen walked up to one of them and began to stroke it.

'Which horse would you like to ride, Femi?'

'I don't know; I've never ridden a horse.'

The Queen was genuinely stunned by Femi's admission: Really! You know how to fight a hundred men yet you can't ride a horse.'

'I've never had the opportunity.'

'Well that changes today, Femi. Today you'll ride with me. Here, go to that horse over there,' she said, staring at a horse opposite her. As instructed Femi went over to the horse.

'Now Femi do exactly what I do. Firstly, we mount like this.' She ran at the horse, grabbed its mane, and swung herself up onto its back. Femi followed suit.

'Comfortable?' Queen Amanirenas asks Femi.

'I'm comfortable.'

'Good, then it's time to ride. I hope you can keep up.' The Queen shouted '*Ayah!*' and slapped a loop of reins on either side of her horse's neck. The horse then galloped off. Femi followed suit with an '*Ayah!*' of his own.

Femi followed Queen Amanirenas into a village outside of the palace. As they rode he observed how the people they came across waved to the Queen and wished them well as they rode past. Femi could clearly see that she was not just respected but she was loved and adored by her people in equal measure.

As they rode on, Femi saw more pyramids. He also saw the temples of Maharraqa and el-Derr, and the fortress known as Qasr Ibrim.

'Enjoying the ride, Femi?' Queen Amanirenas asked.

'Yes I am, my Queen.'

'Excellent! We'll soon be arriving at our destination, Femi. Just hang on tight.'

Sometime later Queen Amanirenas told her horse to hold. The horse came to a standstill. Femi's horse stopped alongside.

'We've arrived, Femi,' the Queen said, dismounting. 'Welcome to the River Nile. The river contains the purest water in the land.' She reached into the river and sampled some of it.

'Come, drink with me. In this heat it's important that we keep ourselves hydrated.'

Femi joined the queen and drank from the river. 'Where I come from, when people talk about this part of the world they mean Egypt. But they never mention the Kush Kingdom.'

'It's because Egypt has closer ties with the Romans.'

'You mean Mark Antony?'

'Yes, Femi. We'll go down the Nile tomorrow to go and see Cleopatra in Egypt. But it's not going to be easy to convince the Egyptians to join us. So we'll have to take care if we want to win favour from them. But that task awaits us tomorrow. For now let's rest. Come, let's enjoy the view.'

Femi and Queen Amanirenas sat down for a while.

'Cleopatra and I would often come here with our families, to play when we were children,' Queen Amanirenas recalled to Femi.

'You know Cleopatra really well, then?'

'Indeed I do Femi. We grew up together. She was very supportive when my brother died. She was there for me.'

'I'm sorry to hear your brother died. How *did* he die, if you don't mind me asking, Queen Amanirenas?'

'It was during one of our early encounters with the Romans. They came to our land and threatened our people with slavery. We fought back and stopped their invasion. But the battle came at a great cost. Many lives were lost, including my brother's. He had been the King, so I became Queen of our people, and I swore I would fight off anyone who threatened our people with slavery or conquest ever again.'

'What was your brother like?'

'He was strong, noble and wise. He ruled our people well. He never looked down on anybody, and he protected us at all costs. Every day I look to his example; very often when I have a difficult decision to make I often wonder what my brother would have done.'

'You're a great queen, O Amanirenas. You're respected by your people. You honour his memory.

'Thank you, Femi.'

'It's a shame I never had a chance to meet your brother. He sounds like a great man.'

'Indeed he was Femi, indeed he was.'

A tear flowed from Queen Amanirenas' eye.

Seeing this, Femi placed his hand on her left shoulder: 'Are you ok?'

Reciprocating Femi's gesture, Queen Amanirenas leaned into Femi and rested her head on his shoulder.

'I am, Femi. I always get emotional when I have a chance to think about my brother.'

'I understand.'

'So, tell me about your story Femi. I can see you're a great warrior; you've obviously been well trained. You are brave and humble, but I don't know much else. I mean, where do you come from? How did you get here?'

'It's a very long and complicated story. I'm not sure you'd believe me.'

'Try me,' Queen Amanirenas said, still resting her head on his shoulder.

'My family's originally from Nigeria – that's in West Africa.'

'West Africa, really? I've never been there before.'

'You should go. It's as beautiful as this place. However, my family and me live in a city called London; it's in England, far to the north of Rome.'

'How did you end up going from Nigeria to England?'

'My parents went there thinking that they could give us a better life. They made a lot of sacrifices and to a certain degree they achieved their aim.'

'Yet from your tone I sense that all is not well in England.'

'Growing up in England as someone who is not white was not easy. We experienced hatred, discrimination, and worst of all racism.'

'Racism?'

'Yes Queen Amanirenas; where I come from you can be targeted physically and verbally simply because of the colour of your skin. Black people have to work harder than everyone else just to stand a chance. Even then, sometimes that isn't enough. There is an order and a system established. It's not set up to favour anyone who isn't white.'

'This is awful. How do you manage to grow up in such a society, Femi?'

'Hustle, work and do what you need to do to survive.'

'So what was it that drove you to go on this quest?'

'Here's where it gets complicated.' Femi paused for a moment. He was worried that if he explained to her that he was from the future and was travelling back in time to rewrite history then she would think he was crazy, and he would lose the trust that he had built up in her. There was also a deeper reason. Femi was beginning to develop feelings for Queen Amanirenas and didn't want to hurt her. So he decided to tell her as much as he could, leaving out the part about time travel.

'I met a man who said he could help me change history. He said he could help me ensure that slavery never came to be. At first I dismissed him. Then my sister was attacked due to the racism I was telling you about. I believe my mission can stop what happened to my sister from ever occurring again. He sent me on various journeys around the world to stop certain events from ever taking place, and the result of that will change our history forever.'

'A very fascinating account and a worthy quest you have, Femi. But I have more questions: Who is this man, and how does he know where to send you?'

'Let's just say that he has divine intervention.'

'Divine intervention. Is he some sort of God?'

'Sort of.'

'Which one? Tell me, Femi!'

'I'm not sure, Queen Amanirenas. He came to me as a person like you and me. As to his true nature, I couldn't tell you.'

'Well divine intervention or not, I'm very glad that you're here. Wherever your mission takes you I'll fight by your side.'

'Likewise, Queen, likewise.'

Queen Amanirenas snuggled up to Femi. Femi gently brushed her hair to one side to get a good look at her. As he gazed into her eyes he smiled at her. Queen Amanirenas smiled back at him.

'You're a very beautiful person, inside and out,' he said.

'The feeling's mutual, Femi.'

'Is there a husband waiting for you back in the palace?'

'No there isn't. Being a ruler and protector of the land can be quite a lonely job.'

'You don't need to be alone any longer.'

During this exchange Queen Amanirenas and Femi could not stop staring at each other. Femi began to move in for a kiss.

But at the very last moment the Queen interrupted by saying, 'We should head back. My soldiers may have returned.' She sprang back onto her feet, dusted herself down and prepared to get back on her horse.

A confused and disappointed Femi responded, 'Of course, Queen Amanirenas,' and also prepared to ride again.

As Femi leapt back onto his horse the queen told him, 'I like spending time with you, Femi. I'm comfortable around you and you make me feel happy. We'll resume whatever this is later, when the time's right. But first let's complete the mission.'

'Whatever you say, Queen Amanirenas.' They both rode back to her palace to get ready to head to Egypt.

Chapter 24: Forming the alliance

The next day Femi, alongside Queen Amanirenas and her guards, went to Egypt to speak with Cleopatra. Upon their arrival at her palace her royal entourage came to greet them.

General Apollodorus, one of her chief advisors, greeted them all personally: 'Welcome back to Egypt, Queen Amanirenas. It's been a very long time since we last saw you.

'It's good to see you too, General.'

'What brings you to Egypt?'

'We need to speak with Queen Cleopatra. We're in need of her help.'

'No problem; I'm sure she'll be only too happy to see you. Come with me.'

Queen Amanirenas, Femi and their entourage followed Apollodorus into the palace. They were escorted into Cleopatra's throne room.

'My Queen, you have visitors.'

Cleopatra rose from her throne to greet them. Many men had been infatuated with her, and it was easy to see why. She was naturally beautiful, and had an elegant presence that made everyone sit up and take notice when she was in the room.

'Amanirenas, my sister, it's good to see you.'

Queen Amanirenas and Cleopatra warmly embraced each other, like long-lost sisters.

'My dear Cleo, still looking radiant as ever, I see. We're in dire need of your help.'

'Please, Amanirenas, come with me.'

'Femi and Adon, come with us. Everyone else, wait here,' Queen Amanirenas instructed her attendants.

They went into Cleopatra's throne room, followed by Apollodorus.

'Tell me, sister,' said Cleopatra. 'How can I help you?'

'It's about the Romans.'

'Have they attacked the Kush Kingdom again?'

'No they haven't. But they did send someone to try to assassinate me. Femi was on hand to stop him.'

Cleopatra turned to Femi and said, 'Thank you for being there to protect my sister. A friend of Amanirenas is a friend of ours. The Egyptians are here for you if you ever need us.'

'I'm humbled to be welcomed by your people – and I may need to take you up on that sooner than you might think.'

'Really? Tell me about how we could be of assistance,' Cleopatra said.

Queen Amanirenas explained: 'It's to do with the reason for us being here. We have long wanted to take out the Romans when the time was right, in retaliation for their attacks on us. We've learned that right now the Romans are at their Games, and we want to take the fight to them. Too many civilisations have suffered at the hands of the Romans. They conquer and enslave people. Forcing them from their homes and making them live a life of poverty and cruelty. The last time we faced the Romans we held them off and pushed them back. But if you were to fight by our side we'd end their rule for ever. Will you join our cause?'

Cleopatra was stunned by the request. She didn't know how to respond.

'This is a great ask. Out of all the things you could have asked of me I'd never have expected this.'

'I wouldn't have asked if there was no other way, Cleopatra. But this is incredibly important. The Romans are a plague in this world and need to be dealt with.'

'The Romans can't be conquered. Almost everyone they've ever faced they've destroyed.'

'Except *us*,' Queen Amanirenas countered. 'Don't you see? The reason why the Romans haven't come back is because they're genuinely afraid of us. They faced a force that was every bit as scary and intimidating as they are. If that's what we can do by ourselves, think what we could do if you fought by our side!'

Cleopatra got up from her throne and stood with her back turned to everyone. She was unable to look Queen Amanirenas in the eye.

'Amanirenas, I empathise with your plight. But on this I can't help you.'

'But why? You've never turned your back on me before. You were one of the first people to reach out to me when the Romans had attacked previously, and gave me moral support. Why now?'

'It's simple. She's in love with a Roman,' Femi asserted.

'*What?*' General Apollodorus yelled. 'How dare you? You barge into our palace and make such accusations. How *dare* you?'

'But it's true. That's why she's hesitant.'

Trying to calm the situation down, General Adon said, 'Femi, this is a very serious accusation. Do you have proof of this?'

'The proof is right in front of us, isn't it, Queen Cleopatra?' He got up and walked towards her. 'Look, it wasn't my intention to bring this up. That's not why I'm here. You have a right to love whoever your heart desires. All I'm here to do is save lives. My mission is to end slavery. I've been to different parts of the world trying to rid the world of this disease. Too many lives have been damaged by it. It's not acceptable for a human being to live a terrible life simply because of the colour of their skin. Defeating the Romans will end all of this, and enable us to build a better world for everyone.

'If you're worried about Mark Antony,' he continued, 'you can speak to him. Perhaps get him on our side. But with or without you, Caesar's got to go. And we'd have a much better chance of success with Egypt fighting alongside us.'

Cleopatra shed a tear at Femi's words. She turned round to face him. 'Your mission is just. I can tell that you're an honourable man, Femi. But even if I wanted to fight alongside you – let's say for a moment I could convince Mark Antony to join us – slavery is a way of life in this part of the world. Without our slaves we wouldn't have been able to construct the world that we have today.'

'There's a difference between a trusted worker and a slave. A trusted worker is an ally who'll work for you happily – and more importantly, work for you willingly. They work in the knowledge that they're treated fairly and have a chance of a good life. Slaves, on the other hand, are forced to work against their will. They're mistreated and have no option of living a life of their own. This is what causes them to rise up and rebel. What would you rather have, Cleopatra? Do you want workers that will willingly work for you, or do you want workers that are plotting to kill you behind your back simply because you didn't treat them right? The choice is yours, Cleopatra.'

Reflecting upon this, Cleopatra said, 'The Egyptians will help you in your fight against Rome. We'll also change our ways to make sure that no one will be forced into slavery. We'll create a society that encourages equal opportunity and a chance to earn a living the right way.'

'Thank you, Queen Cleopatra.'

'I'll do all this on one condition, Femi. Let me talk to Mark Antony first. He's due to come here tonight.'

'As you wish, Queen Cleopatra,' said Femi, nodding.

As he started to walk away Cleopatra asked him: 'Femi, how did you know about me and Mark Antony?'

'When you have travelled the world as much as I have,' said Femi, 'you meet different people and after a while you learn how to read them. The look in your eyes was one of love. That's how I knew.'

Femi, General Adon and Queen Amanirenas left the throne room.

General Apollodorus stayed behind and then approached Cleopatra, disappointed in what he had just learned: 'Of all the people you could have fallen for, why Mark Antony? What are you going to do?'

'I love him, but I have a duty to my people. Sooner or later the Romans will try to add Egypt to their empire. Too long we have mistreated foreigners. How would you feel if you were forced into bondage all your life? We can correct those wrongs with their help. I'll speak to Mark Antony when he comes tonight.'

'Despite this, you're my Queen. I'll stand by you, and I'll be here for you if you need me.'

'Thank you, General.'

Outside the throne room Femi, General Adon and Queen Amanirenas debated what had just happened. Femi had his doubts about whether Cleopatra would keep her promise: 'Can we trust Cleopatra to keep her word?'

'Cleopatra is a woman of great virtue. She will help us on this,' said Queen Amanirenas.

General Adon also had his own concerns over this: 'I share Femi's concerns, my Queen. This is a very delicate matter. Mark Antony could easily tell Caesar, and that would wreck everything.'

'I've known Cleopatra my whole life. She has always come through when I've needed her most.'

'I hope you're right, my Queen. I hope you're right.'

As night fell, Mark Antony rode into Egypt with two of his guards.

General Apollodorus was waiting for him: 'Mark Antony; welcome back to Egypt. Cleopatra has been expecting you. Step this way.'

'Thank you, General. Guards, wait here. I'll return shortly.'

General Apollodorus escorted Mark Antony to the throne room: 'Queen Cleopatra, your guest has arrived.'

'Thank you, Apollodorus. Please leave us. I'll take it from here.'

'Of course, my Queen.' General Apollodorus left Mark Antony and Cleopatra to talk.

The moment he had left the room Mark Antony rushed over to Cleopatra in excitement and kissed her.

'At long last! It's felt like an eternity since I last saw your beauty at first hand.' Hugging her tightly, he sensed that she was troubled. 'Is something wrong, my love?'

'Please sit, we need to talk.'

Mark was understandably concerned by Cleopatra's behaviour: 'What's wrong, my love? Please tell me – I've never seen you look so distressed.'

'I had a visit from Queen Amanirenas today.'

'The ruler of the Kush Kingdom?'

'Yes.'

'Is she all right?'

'She is.'

'Ok, why was she here?'

'She wanted my help.'

'Help with what? Relax, you can tell me.' Mark Antony took Cleopatra's hand in an attempt to reassure her.

'As you were aware, many years ago the Romans attacked her kingdom. Even though she fought them off she's seen the Romans continue to build their empire elsewhere and enslave many populations. She plans to ...'

'Tell me, Cleopatra! What's going on?'

'The Kush Kingdom plans to attack the Romans during the Games, and she's asked me to lend the armies of Egypt to her cause. I've agreed to help her.'

'You've agreed to do *what*?' Mark Antony stormed out of his chair, fuming. 'You want to attack my home. You want to attack my empire and my ruler. How dare you?'

'Don't you see, this is a chance for us to be free? We can rid the world of Caesar once and for all. Caesar has been a curse upon the world. With him dead, many people would be free.'

'You're asking me to turn my back on my friend, Cleopatra.'

'So he's your friend now, is he? You weren't thinking about that when you were in my bed.'

A perplexed Mark snapped back, 'I've risked everything for you. My career, my status and my home. I've put it all on the line for you. And this is how you repay my love!'

'Stay with me, Mark,' Cleopatra pleaded as she placed a loving hand on his cheek. 'Don't go back to Rome. I asked Amanirenas to let me speak to you first to give me a chance to save you. Stay here and be safe. Think about how many people have been enslaved and conquered by the Romans. You're always telling me about the horrors you've witnessed during the expansion of the Roman Empire. Together we can undo the damage that has been done by all of this. For too long we've benefited whilst others have been enslaved and made to suffer in bondage.

'We have to be better than this,' she continued. 'Rule by my side and make the world a better place for everyone. And not just for everyone living today, but for centuries to come. If we let Caesar live this change will never happen. No one should ever be a slave to anyone.' Cleopatra leaned over to give Mark Antony a kiss.

At the last second Mark Antony stopped her and moved backwards: 'I'm sorry, Cleopatra. I can't do this, I can't. I need to go – *now!* Caesar must be warned.' He turned, and ran out of the throne room.

'Mark, Mark!' shouted Cleopatra, to no avail. Mark had decided to choose duty over his love, to the detriment of both the Kush Kingdom and Egypt. The mission was now in danger of being sabotaged.

Chapter 25: Stopping Mark Antony

Disgusted by what he had just heard from Cleopatra, Mark Antony went outside. He couldn't believe what she had just told him. Mark simply couldn't get around the fact that to stop slavery and save millions of people from suffering in the future Julius Caesar and his empire would have to come to an end. He slumped to his feet and covered his face with his head in his hands; he did not know what to do next.

Two of Mark's generals were waiting outside Cleopatra's chambers, and they saw that he was in distress. Concerned by his plight, they ran over towards him.

'My lord, you are you all right?' they asked.

'Yes, I am. We have to go. We have to leave immediately. We must warn Caesar. He's in grave danger.'

'My Lord, we'll go at once.'

Mark and his guards walked swiftly out of Cleopatra's palace. As they were about to mount their horses Femi was there to meet them.

'I had a feeling that Cleopatra wouldn't be able to change your mind. So I've been waiting here just in case.'

'You!' Mark Antony yelled. 'This is *your* fault. I don't know where you've come from, but since you've got here Cleopatra's changed. She used to be free, innocent and without a care in the world. With her I felt at peace. She wasn't interested in war, politics or conquest. She was happy to be in love with me. But now she's talking about murdering my best friend.'

Mark's guards attacked Femi. But Femi was now a seasoned fighter, his skills sharpened through the hardships he had faced on his journey. He quickly disarmed them. He did not wish to kill them, though. He hoped that there might still be a chance that Mark Antony would be open to reason. So instead he knocked both of the men out cold.

Then he approached Mark with his sword in attack mode. Mark drew his sword, too. They circled each other like a predator circles his prey in the wild.

Sensing that there could still be a chance to avoid further conflict, Femi tried to reason with Mark Antony. 'Listen to me, Mark. I don't wish to fight you. In your heart, I know you're a good man. You're a man of reason. What I'm about to tell you may seem like fantasy, but I need you to listen to what I have to say. My name's Femi Adebayo. I'm not from this timeline. I'm from the future.'

'What do you mean, you're from the future? What kind of trick is this?'

'This is no trick, I assure you. I'm speaking the truth. I come from a time period many generations from now. In the future, generations of people all over the world will suffer. People will be taken from their homes; they will be raped, beaten and even slaughtered. Cultures will be erased and many people will never ever see their homelands again. People will be forced into slavery. Slavery will become a curse; slavery will spread like a virus and will become a disease that will engulf this planet.'

Mark said, 'There's nothing new here, Femi. Slavery already exists. Even as we speak slaves are being brought into Rome to serve our empire. Slavery's a way of life here, Femi. Look around you. Look at Egypt. You see all those pyramids in the desert how do you think they were built? They were built by slaves.'

'No, Mark, this is where you're wrong. They were built by free men; good men built those pyramids through their own sweat and tears. Men like you and me.'

Mark hesitated. He lowered his sword. 'Tell me one thing, Femi. If you're from the future, why did you come here? Of all the places that you could have gone to, why did you come to this time period?'

Femi lowered his sword as well. 'To be honest with you, Mark, for a long time I've wondered that myself. I've made many journeys during this quest.

I've faced fearsome adversaries and beasts, I've had to take down entire armies. I've had to save men from the brink of death. Each of those journeys could've been the end of me. But each journey, I survived. With each survival I gained knowledge, I gained growth. But they always felt like they weren't the end. They always felt like they were simply the beginning. That's it.'

Mark, puzzled, said, 'That's *what*?'

Femi looked at Mark and smiled. 'At last I know why my mission has to end here. Every ending has to have a beginning. This is the root. This is where slavery really took hold internationally. The Roman Empire had such an effect on the world. It influenced so many things: warfare, mathematics, the sciences and medicine. The beneficial effects of the Roman Empire will be felt by many for generations to come. However its effects also include slavery. Think about it. From the way some slaves are treated as pets to people having to kill each other in your arenas for entertainment. It all began here.'

Mark paused for a moment and had a deep think about what Femi had just told him. 'There's truth in what you say. The Roman Empire's the most dominant empire in the world right now. We've had a major say in matters affecting tens of thousands of people. Perhaps we can change our ways and make the world a better space, and spare the future from the horrors that you mentioned. But I ask you this:

Why does this have to involve killing Julius Caesar?'

Femi, with a heavy heart, explained, 'You probably won't like this, but Caesar is seen as the all-conquering hero. He's the symbol that will encourage others to conquer lands that are not their own and enslave the populace that they conquer. With Caesar gone, the message is sent that conquering and slaving people won't be allowed. It isn't about stopping Caesar himself. It *is* about stopping the people who'd otherwise come after him and emulate him.'

'Caesar's ambitious,' said Mark Antony. 'But he's a good man. If we didn't conquer other countries and build our empire we'd stand still – and that'd leave us weak and vulnerable. Our enemies would strike out at us. But most of all Caesar's my friend. I can't betray him. I'm sorry, Femi, you're a noble man and your intentions are pure. Under different circumstances I'd have lent my sword to your cause. Under different circumstances we'd be allies. But I can't kill Caesar. I just can't.'

'I'm not asking you to,' responded Femi. 'Just to stay out of our way and let us do what needs to be done.'

'Then let me go, Femi.'

'If I let you go, you and your guards would go and warn Caesar. I can't let that happen.'

'You're right; I *would* go and warn Caesar.'

'So where does this leave us, Mark?'

'I think you know, Femi.' With regret Mark raised his sword again and went into his combat stance. 'I'm sorry, Femi, but if you wish to kill Caesar then you're going to have to kill me first.'

'I'm sorry as well, Mark; I wish it didn't have to come down to this.' Femi raised his sword as well. Deep down, he'd known that this was going to be the most likely outcome. He had faced so many opponents during his mission, but this time things were different. Everybody else he had ever fought he had had to fight, as they were either on the side of evil and/or purposely enslaving people. But all Mark was doing was standing by his friend. It was a very admirable quality.

The two warriors circled each other, both staring each other down in an attempt to psych out their opponent. Mark Antony made the first move, a left-sided thrust, which Femi easily blocked. Mark Antony came at Femi again, and again Femi blocked him. This pattern continued for a while.

'Fight me, you coward!' Mark Antony shouted at Femi.

'I don't want to fight you. It's not too late. Help us end this. Slavery's a curse on this world. It is a disease that's ruined the lives of too many people. Help us end this.'

'I can't kill Caesar. I can't stand by and let this happen.'

'Then you leave me with no choice, Mark. You've had your chance.'

At that moment Femi knew what he had to do. Now was not the time for him to show weakness. In full fury he went into the attack. He went at Mark Antony with the speed, venom and ferociousness that had been crucial in overcoming the Portuguese invasion in 15th-century West Africa, and in saving Nat Turner from death. At first, Mark Antony was able to match Femi blow for blow. But as the battle went on Mark Antony found himself on the back foot. Then Femi slashed Mark Antony just above his right knee. Feeling the pain of the cut Mark Antony fell onto the other knee. Femi backtracked, but maintained his battle stance, ready to resume if required: 'It's over. Surrender, Mark, or I swear I'll kill you. This is your last chance.'

'Romans never surrender!' was Mark Antony's response. He let out a howl, then got up and went after Femi again in a fit of rage. Mark was out of control, swiping left, right and centre. There was no coordination, no strategy and no thought – and he was playing into Femi's hands.

Femi continued to duck and dive all Mark Antony's sword-swings. Femi eventually managed to block, and unleashed a spinning left elbow straight into Mark Antony's jaw. Then Femi delivered a quick one-two punch combination, and sent Mark Antony flying down onto the ground with a backflip kick. Mark Antony landed head first.

He was beaten. The fight was over. But just like an over-the-hill boxer who never knows when to quit, he groggily tried to get back up onto his feet to resume the battle. He managed to get back up onto one knee. When he did, he saw a figure standing in front of him. It was his love, Cleopatra.

'It's over, Mark,' she said as she held out her hand to him. Mark accepted. Once Cleopatra had helped Mark to his feet she did the unthinkable. She stabbed him. Coughing out blood and staring directly into her eyes, Mark Antony heard the last words she would ever say to him: 'I love you.'

Mark died in her arms. Queen Amanirenas, her guards and some of Cleopatra's men came onto the scene. Queen Amanirenas looked at Femi and saw that he was dumbfounded. She turned to Cleopatra and saw the tears dropping from her eyes – she had made the impossible choice. To save the world from slavery and protect generations of people to come, the love of her life had to die.

Femi tried to reach out to Cleopatra 'Queen Cleopatra, I'm ...'

She brushed his hand aside and shouted, 'Are you happy? Are you happy now? Is this what you wanted?'

'Queen Cleopatra, I tried to talk to him. I tried to tell him to stop fighting, but he wouldn't listen to me.'

Queen Amanirenas interjected, 'Cleopatra, I'm truly sorry for your loss. But this is not Femi's fault. He did everything possible to avoid killing Mark Antony.'

Cleopatra called Apollodorus and said, 'Prepare the armies. Tomorrow we'll march to Rome and end this. Mark Antony's sacrifice won't be in vain. We'll rid the world of slavery. Queen Amanirenas, tell your troops to prepare to move out in the morning.'

Queen Amanirenas nodded in agreement. 'Of course, Cleopatra. Is there anything more we can do?'

'Just leave me alone,' Cleopatra responded tearfully. Everyone left her to hold her beloved for the final time. They knew that she needed time to grieve. They knew that they needed to give her space.

Chapter 26: The voyage to Rome

The next day Femi and Queen Amanirenas gathered the armies of Egypt and the Kush Kingdom. Together they planned their assault on the Roman Empire. Viewing an old map of Italy they formulated their strategy to beat the Romans.

General Aton had spotted a route into Rome which would enable them to strike at the heart of the Roman Empire.

'Based on what I see in this map, the River Tiber runs through the very centre of Rome. Its mouth is where we should disembark from our ships. With the Romans distracted by the Games it won't be as heavily guarded as usual. We'll land there and march east to the centre of the city. This is where we'll find the Coliseum, the centrepiece of the Roman Empire. Striking them there will deliver a blow they'll never recover from.'

Queen Amanirenas said, 'I agree. All the key figures of the Roman Empire will be there, especially Caesar. We can eliminate them in one go. This is too good a chance to waste.'

'Where are slaves normally kept in the Roman Empire?' Femi asked.

'It varies, Femi. It depends on whether they're owned by a household or trained as gladiators. Although I do hear rumours of a small slave market a few miles away from the Coliseum.'

'We need to head there first.'

'Why? The Coliseum needs to be our focus point. That is where our enemy will be, and it's the key to our victory.'

'You're right, Aton. But I have a promise to keep. Just give me handful of men. When I arrive I'll head to the market first and then I'll go to the Coliseum to join you. There's someone I promised I would return home if he's still alive.'

General Aton looked at Queen Amanirenas. She nodded to grant Femi permission to carry out his side mission.

'Okay, Femi,' said Aton. 'We'll give you two dozen of our best men. Make sure you succeed in your quest and return to us for the attack. You started this; you need to be there to finish it.'

'Thank you, General Aton.'

'Where's Cleopatra? She should be informed of our plans. We need to have her buy in on this.'

'If it's my support you need, then it's my support you have,' said Cleopatra, emerging from the crowd to join the others in the discussion. They were surprised to see her, as it was only the day before that she had lost the love of her life. An awkward silence fell. Nobody knew how best to greet her.

In an attempt to break the silence, Queen Amanirenas spoke first: 'Cleopatra, how are …?'

But Cleopatra interrupted her, saying: 'General Aton, how sure are you of this plan succeeding?'

'This is our best chance of victory, Queen Cleopatra. It's also the one with the minimum risk. Attacking them whilst the Games are on will allow us to catch them off guard.'

'Very well; whatever you need from us, Egypt will provide. We'll give our orders to the armies and prepare to set sail. Let's get to it!'

'You heard Cleopatra; get going!' shouted General Aton.

'Femi,' said Cleopatra. 'May I have a moment of your time please?'

'Of course, Queen Cleopatra,' said Femi, walking up to her.

'About yesterday: I know you tried to save Mark Antony and did everything you could to stop him from dying. I believe in your purpose and your mission. However, know this. If this mission doesn't succeed, if this plan fails, know that I will hold you accountable. Failure's not an option. I won't let Mark Antony die for nothing. If the mission dies, you'll die with it. Is that clear?'

'Understood,' responded Femi. He and Cleopatra shared an intense stare-down at each other.

'Good. I'll see you on the battlefield,' said Cleopatra, then went off to prepare her troops for the voyage and the upcoming battle.

Queen Amanirenas, noting his tension, went up to Femi: 'Are you all right?'

'I'm fine, my Queen.'

'What was that all about?'

'Cleopatra was just making her feelings clear about the whole situation. It's nothing to worry about. Let's ready the troops.'

The Egyptians and the Kush Kingdom then gathered their armies. They set sail for Rome at noon. Femi was on the same ship as Queen Amanirenas. After the fleet had been sailing for several days, for the last night of their voyage the ships anchored near an island to give the men some rest. Femi found himself alone. Finding it difficult to sleep, he went to the upper deck of the ship, looked out at the sea and began to ponder on the meaning of this battle. This was the final part of his mission; if the Kush Kingdom and the Egyptians came out on top, slavery would be no more.

Then Femi thought back to the places he had been to, and began to piece together what each of his earlier missions meant in itself. His mission in West Africa had ended up saving the peoples of Africa from slavery. His mission to save Nat Turner was really about stopping a civil war that would have seen blood spilled everywhere; slavery had simply been a trigger point for it. His mission aboard the Fredensborg had helped prevent transatlantic slavery from taking place. His mission in Rome was the final piece of the complicated puzzle that Mr Diggity had put together; success in Rome would stamp out slavery at its point of origin in the western world.

As Femi was deep in his thoughts, he heard a reassuring voice, one he had come to adore. 'Having trouble sleeping, Femi?'

As Femi turned around he saw Queen Amanirenas. 'A little bit, my Queen. I came out here to do some thinking.'

'What were you thinking about? Is it to do with what Cleopatra said to you before we set sail?'

'No – it's more than that.'

Queen Amanirenas had grown fond of Femi during their time together, and was beginning to worry for him. To help put him at ease she walked up to him and gently placed her hands on his shoulders.

'Talk to me, Femi; what's wrong? You haven't been yourself since we sailed.'

'I've been thinking about my mission. I've been wondering what my mission has meant. I've also been thinking about my future. If we succeed, the world's going to change, and not just in the here and now but for generations to come. I mean, I've been trained to be a warrior. What purpose does a warrior have in the world when there isn't a war to fight or a battle to win?'

'Maybe it'll be time for you to rest,' she suggested.

'Me, rest? I don't know the meaning of the word.'

'Femi, ever since I've met you all I've seen you do is fight, fight, fight some more and continue to fight. You've been bearing the burden on your shoulders for so long. When we succeed you'll not need to carry it any more. Your mission will be complete. So instead of fighting, why not concentrate on creating a future where you will be happy? A future where you can be happy with me?'

She provocatively sat on Femi's lap. But he said, 'Queen Amanirenas, I'm not sure I know what you mean by your last comment.'

'I told you, we'll resume this when the time's right. And now's the time, Femi. I haven't been totally honest with you, especially since what almost occurred between us at the River Nile. Then I was putting my duty to my people first. But now I need to do what's right for my heart. It's lonely ruling my people by myself. You've earned the trust and respect of everyone in the Kush Kingdom. I offer you a place on my throne. Rule beside me as their King.'

Femi was taken aback by her offer. 'Look, Queen Amanirenas; you know how I feel about you. You've known that for a long time. But it isn't that simple I'm due to go back to where I come from when this is all over. I can't stay, I can't ...'

Queen Amanirenas kissed Femi, stopping his words.

Then she said, 'Think about what I just said. I've opened my heart to you, Femi. What you do with it is up to you. I'll be waiting for you in my cabin.'

Queen Amanirenas stared at Femi and winked at him as if to suggest she was his if he wanted her, then she seductively swayed her way back down to the lower deck.

Femi smiled as she walked away. But his smile turned to annoyance when a stern voice said: 'Why is it whenever a pretty girl flutters her eyes men forget about what they're meant to be doing and are only too quick to drop their trousers?'

'That can only be Mr Diggity, showing up when you're not wanted,' quipped Femi.

'I show up when you *need* me to show up, not when you *want* me to show up. They're two different things. What are you thinking?'

'What do you mean?'

'You know what I mean; you were about to go downstairs and get some. Boy, you're on the verge of finishing what you started. Everything you have done so far has led up to this. You've fought through lions, armies and bastard captains, and you want to risk it all for a one night stand.'

'She isn't some piece of skirt, Mr Diggity. It's more than that. I …'

'Don't even go there. Just think about this. How would it work? Once all this is done, you have a future to return to, remember.'

'What if I don't return?'

'That's not part of the deal, Femi. Look, I know you have strong feelings for the Queen. She's a remarkable woman. Under different circumstances I'd be saying *let me know when the wedding is*. But now isn't the time. Boy, I'd be happy for you to find love. But she isn't the one. You have a job to do tomorrow. Tomorrow you're going to have to face down what's arguably one of the greatest empires that history has ever known. If your head's not in the game or if you're even one per cent off your very best, all that you've gone through will have been for nothing. You still have a sister to save, remember – or have you forgotten that too, because your puppy dog eyes have been wandering elsewhere?'

'Thanks for the tip, Mr Diggity. Now, piss off.'

'Don't say I didn't warn you, Femi. Don't say I didn't warn you. You have a mission to finish. Don't fuck it up now.' Mr Diggity stormed off, back to the future.

Femi took some time to calm down from Mr Diggity's scolding. Then he headed down to the lower deck to look for Queen Amanirenas. She would be waiting in her cabin …

He knocked. 'Come in,' she said. Femi walked in and closed the door behind him. Queen Amanirenas turned round, relieved it was Femi.

Worried that she might have unsettled him, she said, 'Look, Femi, I'm sorry for coming onto you like that, but …'

He walked up to Queen Amanirenas and placed a finger on her lips. Then he kissed her. After a brief stare-down they began kissing each other passionately, then started taking off each other's clothes, while caressing each other tightly. Femi picked up Queen Amanirenas and carried her onto her bed. They spent the night making love passionately to one another as though the next day would be their last.

Chapter 27: The mission to end all missions

At the crack of dawn Queen Amanirenas was beginning to awaken. Making love to Femi had put her into a state of warmth and happiness that she didn't think was possible. Reaching out with her right arm she was expecting to cop a feel of the new man in her life. But instead of Femi's warm body all she found was an empty space on the bed. She moved her arm around, clutching different parts of the bed. Realising that her hero was no longer beside her, she sat up and looked around.

'It's dawn. Knowing him, he's probably out training.' She got out of bed to wash and get changed to go and find her lover. Soon afterwards she went back to the upper deck in search of him. Predictably he was there, practising his swordplay and fighting skills. He wanted to ensure that he was sharp and in condition mentally and physically to battle the Romans.

When Femi had finished his workout he had his back turned to her. Queen Amanirenas approached and, cuddling him around his waist, she reached round and kissed him on his cheek: 'Hey, lover, how are you today?'

'I'm well, my Queen,' Femi responded, still focused on the battle ahead.

'My, my, someone got out the wrong side of my bed this morning. I hope you don't regret last night. I enjoyed myself and I thought you did too.'

Femi turned to Queen Amanirenas and kissed her on the lips. 'No regrets – but within a few hours we're going to face the Romans. I need to be ready. Many people have sacrificed a lot to get us here – Mark Antony and Cleopatra especially. We've come too far to let it all go to waste. After the battle we'll figure out where we go next. Until then we need to concentrate on the mission. Anyway, the troops will soon awaken, so let's try to act professionally.' Femi stroked her hair and kissed her one more time.

'Very well, Femi. I'll see you on the battlefield.' She left Femi to prepare the troops.

As Femi turned round, General Aton was waiting for him with a big smirk on his face.

'What?' Femi asked.

General Aton, knowing full well what had been going on, played along with Femi. 'Nothing. The Roman shore is upon us; ready to prepare for our landing, lover boy?'

Femi, laughing, said, 'Of course General! So, what's the plan?'

A few hours later the Kush Kingdom ships had reached the mouth of the Tiber. As they moored up, a small troop of Roman soldiers noticed their arrival and went to meet them.

'Hold!' one of them said. 'You have many ships. Why have you come here?'

'We bring gifts for Caesar,' General Aton responded.

'What gifts?' the soldier asked.

'This!' As General Aton spoke, a Kush Kingdom soldier fired an arrow into the soldier's head, killing him instantly. With the Roman soldiers surprised, the Kush Kingdom soldiers killed them all within seconds. The first part of the plan was successful.

Femi gathered a handful of men and prepared to head to the slave market to try to fulfil the promise he had made to Mido.

Before he set off, General Aton said, 'Remember, Femi. The reason for choosing this moment to attack was to surprise the Romans. If you fail to return within the hour or if our position is compromised, we'll head to the Coliseum without you.'

'I understand, General. Rest assured I'll be back here to march on the Coliseum. Right, men, follow me; I have a promise to keep.'

Femi and his men headed out in search of the slave market. They searched tirelessly, but to no avail. It was approaching the hour, and soon they would have to return or the Kush Kingdom would begin the march without them.

One of the men said, 'Femi, I know you wish to honour this promise, but we need to head back.

We'll be needed to win this battle. We can continue the search after we've conquered the Romans.'

Femi sighed, but taking into account what was at stake he responded, 'You're right. We'll give it ten more minutes. If we don't find anything then we'll go back.'

'Wait!' shouted one of the soldiers. He pointed out to them a team of horses pulling a wooden cart with slaves chained up inside it.

'Perhaps this is it. We'll free these men,' Femi ordered.

Femi and his warriors charged in and killed the traders transporting the slaves. Then they freed the captives, removing the shackles and making sure that they unchained everyone in sight.

'I don't know who you are, but thank you,' one of the slaves said to Femi.

'You're very welcome. You're free to go. I was wondering, though, if you could help me with one thing. I'm looking for a man named Karim. He's not from around here. He comes from the Kush Kingdom.'

'Why do you seek Karim?' the slave asked.

'I made a promise to his brother to find him and free him if he was still alive.'

'Mido! You know my brother.'

'Yes I do … hang on, he's *your* brother?'

'Yes; I'm Karim. I'm the one you seek!' Karim hugged Femi; he was grateful to Mido for not giving up on him and giving him the chance to gain his freedom.

'I'm honoured to meet you. We'll return you home, but there's one final mission I need to complete first.'

'Final mission; what would that be?'

'To end slavery by destroying the Roman Empire.'

'We'll join you! The sooner we end the Roman Empire the better. What can we do to help you?'

The freed slaves rode back with Femi and his men; after suffering from the Romans and enduring slavery first hand they were going to be only too happy to see Femi and his men complete their mission. The slaves offered to show the army the way to Coliseum. They wanted to see justice done for anyone that had been enslaved. So they rode back to join the armies of the Kush Kingdom. Cleopatra's forces awaited them, too; everything was falling into place. The final battle would soon be upon them, and with it the fate of generations to come.

Meanwhile inside the Coliseum, Caesar and his cohorts were enjoying the Games.

'There's nothing like a good bit of sport to grace this fine arena,' said Caesar. 'Wouldn't you all agree?' His entourage all nodded in agreement with him.

'It's a shame Mark Antony isn't here to see this. He's missing some great sport. Perhaps he's having fun and games with that Cleopatra. I swear that woman will be the death of him unless I kill her first.'

All of a sudden a loud noise echoed over the Coliseum. Footsteps could be heard – many footsteps. They kept getting louder, along with a chant. The competitors stood still. The people in the audience started to look at each other, wondering what on earth was going on.

'What's that noise?' Caesar asked amidst the confusion.

'It sounds like a march,' Brutus responded. 'And they're shouting something.'

The armies of the Kush Kingdom were marching towards the coliseum, chanting '*Freedom, Freedom, Freedom!*' It was more than a chant. It had become their battle cry.

A few yards from the gates of the Coliseum, Femi shouted, 'Light them up!' The archers lit their fire arrows.

'*Fire!*' screamed Femi. The archers shot their arrows into the Coliseum.

As the arrows flew in, Caesar shouted, 'Everyone take cover!' Loud screams soon started echoing around the Coliseum as people were wounded and killed.

'Light them again,' ordered Femi. The archers lit their second set of arrows.

'*Fire!*' Femi barked. More fire arrows were bearing down on everyone in the Coliseum. Sensing that the Romans were now on the back foot, Femi gave the signal to Queen Cleopatra and Queen Amanirenas.

'Attack!' yelled Cleopatra, and the forces of Egypt charged towards the Coliseum.

Queen Amanirenas followed suit; pointing at the Coliseum she yelled. 'Forward!' and the armies of the Kush Kingdom raced towards the Coliseum.

Femi saw that the doors of the Coliseum were sealed. 'Break the doors down!' he ordered. Using the wooden rams that they carried with them the armies bashed them against the doors until they broke down. Then a fury was unleashed upon the Romans – a fury that they had never ever witnessed before. The Romans were used to conquering and dishing out their brand of empowerment. But now it was their turn to be afraid.

Femi, alongside the Egyptians and members of the Kush Kingdom, charged at the Romans. The attackers were fuelled by rage and a sense of injustice; not just for their people but for people all over the world. This was their chance to avenge anyone who had ever been taken into slavery. They had an opportunity to change the world for the better. This was their chance to create a better world for today, tomorrow and for generations to come.

'Attack! Show no mercy, take no prisoners. No mercy and no quarter given. If they have a weapon and they come at us, they die!' Cleopatra shouted. The Romans struggled to contain the fury that was upon them, but it was difficult for them because they were used to being the aggressors and being on the front foot in confrontations.

'Fall back, fall back!' shouted one of the Roman generals.

'*NO!* We're Romans. We don't run from anyone,' Julius Caesar shouted when he heard that command.

'My Lord, if we don't fall back, our army will be slaughtered. We're not prepared for this battle. If we continue here we'll fall, my Lord.'

'I've not built this empire to see it squashed by this filth. We *will* prevail. Tell your army to regroup and go on the attack.'

'But my Lord ...'

'*Now*, General.'

'As you wish, my Lord.'

The general was not pleased with Caesar's response, but soldiers follow orders so he had no choice but to comply with Caesar. The general knew that the Romans were about to be beaten. But Caesar was too stubborn to admit defeat.

Pretty soon the Coliseum was covered with dead Romans. As the armies of Egypt and the Kush Kingdom continued their march through the arena they slaughtered everyone that the Romans threw at them.

Femi spotted an opening. The top of the Coliseum was clear.

'Troops, cover me. I have a message that these people need to hear.' He raced to the top tier of the Coliseum. Leveraging all the skill he had amassed on this mission he dispatched the Roman soldiers blocking his path. He went atop the stairs of the Coliseum and shouted out to everyone: 'STOP!!!'

Just like that, everyone stopped fighting for a moment. Everyone just stared at him as if to say *who is this guy*?

Femi yelled out a battle cry, and shouted, 'Slaves, warriors and fellow oppressed! My name's Femi Adebayo. We're not what you think. We're not your enemy. We're here to help you. We're here on a mission of greater significance and importance. Many of you have been forced into slavery against your will. Many of you were taken away from your families at a young age. You've suffered in silence, you've suffered many injustices. You've been beaten, mistreated and undervalued. Your voice hasn't been heard.

'Well, today all of that ends. Today's the day that'll change the world for ever. Today's the day that we will liberate everyone. Today's the day that we say *No more!* Today's the day that we say *Enough is enough!* Today's the day that we rid the world of slavery. Now I ask you, will join us and end this tyranny?'

After a short silence a Roman soldier turned towards him and shouted, 'Yes, I'm with you!'

Another soldier shouted, 'Your cause is noble and just. I'll gladly fight by your side.'

Soldier after soldier turned to Femi and shouted, 'I'm with you!'

Femi turned to the audience in the Coliseum and said 'Are you with me?'

The people yelled, '*Yes!*'

Femi asked again, even louder, 'Are you with me?'

'YES!' was the emphatic response.

Femi gave a final battle cry: 'Then follow me to victory! Destroy Caesar and his empire.'

When Femi had first come to the Kush Kingdom his mission had been to unite it with Egypt to take down the Romans. Instead he did something even better. He united all three nations by giving them something that slavery had almost removed from them. He gave them hope.

The fighting resumed, because there were still some loyalists to the Roman Empire, but they were now dwarfed by others who had grown sick and tired of being puppets for the Roman aristocrats. Femi stood there and watched all this unfold. He also began to notice one thing; the amount of blood that was being shed. There is no point creating a new world if there is no one around to see it. He knew that if he took down Caesar the fighting would cease immediately.

Femi looked around and saw Caesar surrounded by his guards. Caesar, looking around nervously, spotted Femi. Femi stared him down; Caesar knew he was next. Femi lifted up his sword and made his march towards Caesar. Loyalists of the Roman Empire started coming towards him with their weapons. Femi delivered a roundhouse kick to the first loyalist, then followed up with a superman punch to the second. After a brief sword fight with the third he took him out with an elbow to the face and a leg sweep. After fighting on through many more, his prize was now in sight; Julius Caesar was within reach. Just one thing stood in his way.

Caesar yelled, 'Flamma, protect me!'

Flamma, one of the best gladiators known to history, put on his helmet, picked up his shield and stalked towards Femi. Femi remained calm and got into his battle stance. He thought there might be one last chance to reason with him: 'Hear me, Flamma, I know you feel you have to protect Caesar. But you owe him nothing. I know your history. He may eventually give you freedom, but you were born into slavery from your birth in Gaul like so many of us that stand here. I give you one chance to stand down; join us and help us end slavery for good.'

But Flamma ignored his words and continued on towards him.

Femi yelled, 'Fine – you've had your chance!' He charged at Flamma with his sword and they went toe to toe with each other. Both men swung their swords at each other, continually jostling and jostling, both men looking for an edge, but neither man finding one. In swordplay they were evenly matched. However whilst Femi was more mobile, agile and athletic, Flamma had the edge on him in terms of brute strength. Femi, realising this, flipped back into a defensive stance. He knew if he was going to win this fight he would have to leverage his speed and outmanoeuvre Flamma. Knowing this, an idea came to his mind. He charged at Flamma just as he was about to swing his sword at him. Then

Femi rolled underneath the swing and slashed his leg. Flamma screamed in pain. Femi beat Flamma, unleashing blow after blow, leveraging the striking techniques he learnt on the West Coast of Africa back in the 15th century.

He managed to knock Flamma's helmet off and went on to beat him to a bloody pulp. Before Femi unleashed the final knockout punch he paused; holding his fist a few inches from Flamma's face, he said, 'This is your last chance; you've fought with honour, but stand down now.'

Flamma said, 'I can't do that; I must fight on.' Femi knocked him out cold. He decided not to kill him, out of respect for his qualities as a warrior; he also felt that Flamma might change once this was all over. He regained his breath and turned round. He sensed his mission was coming to an end. His quest had been a long one and now he only had one thing left to do. To kill Caesar.

Femi and Caesar gazed at each other.

Femi said to him, 'It's over; the Roman Empire, the oppression, slavery; all of this ends now. You'll release everyone now.'

Caesar said, 'My empire will never end.' He drew his sword and pointed it at Femi. The final battle of Femi's mission had come. Everything that Femi had fought for had come down to this. This really was winner takes all. And so the battle began. When fighting Flamma, Femi had been fighting raw brute force. But with Caesar it was more like fighting a snake. Caesar's fighting style was aristocratic, silky, smooth and slippery. He even managed to sneak a cut on Femi.

Caesar looked at him and smirked: 'Had enough?'

Femi paused for a moment. He remembered his training in the 15th century, he remembered his mission to save Nat Turner. He thought about all the close shaves he had been through, and he said to himself *now is not the time to fail*. He had come too far to fail now. So he got up and went after Caesar. Using all his might, his skill and everything he had learned, he started to get the upper hand. The jostling continued, then leveraging the striking techniques he had mastered at the beginning of his journey he managed to elbow Caesar in his chest and landed a crushing blow. With one mighty thrust he impaled Caesar.

Caesar dropped to the ground and just stared at Femi. He looked around the Coliseum. His army was on the verge of defeat. Slaves had risen and rebelled against him and were united in ending his rule.

Caesar turned around, looked at Femi and said to him '*Et tu*, Femi, why? What's your purpose here?'

Femi crouched and stared into his eyes. It had taken him a while, but he had fully grasped why taking down the Roman Empire was his final mission. He explained, 'This is the place where it all begins. Your actions have consequences for many generations to come. Slavery, oppression, mistreating people for your own entertainment – it's all begun here, the way you've been going around conquering and invading other countries, robbing people of their way of living. Other conquerors will follow in your footsteps: Genghis Khan, Pizarro, Napoleon, Hitler – they'll all emulate the destruction and hurt that you've begun. With you and your empire gone we can make the world a better place. We can create a world where people don't get forced into slavery, get raped and beaten to satisfy another person's greed. Today we end slavery once and for all. We'll make sure slavery never comes to be. And now you die.'

Lifting up his sword one final time he gave an almighty scream and beheaded Caesar.

Femi couldn't believe what he had just done. Exhausted, and slightly confused but relieved, he dropped his sword. He looked at the ground; all he could see was Caesar's lifeless body and his head just lying there. He grabbed the head, then walked back up to the top of the Coliseum.

One of the soldiers noticed and, pointing, said, 'Look!' Everyone started looking up at the top of the Coliseum. They turned and looked at Femi. Femi, knowing that he had their attention, lifted Caesar's head up for all to see. The remaining loyalists dropped their weapons. It was over.

Then Femi gave a speech. 'Caesar's dead. The Roman Empire's dead. From this moment on, slavery and oppression are over. No more will people be forced to leave their homes; there'll be no more invasion and erosion of culture and people's way of life. I give to you all peace, but most importantly I give to you FREEDOM!'

The people in the Coliseum roared in approval. They also shouted something else: 'KING FEMI, KING FEMI!'

Femi, smiling politely, responded, 'I'm not a king. I'm merely a messenger who came here on a mission to rid the world of the treacherous act that is slavery. Queen Amanirenas and Queen Cleopatra, you will oversee a new rule and new kingdom. This will be a kingdom that will serve the people – and not just the people of the Kush Kingdom, Egypt or Rome but the world. One that will fight the good fight. Wherever there's a hint of oppression or slavery returning you'll be there to snuff it out before it even begins.'

The people in the Coliseum roared in approval. Cleopatra gave him a nod, and Amanirenas looked at Femi and smiled; she looked proud to have fallen for such a noble man. Femi smiled. He had succeeded in his mission. Today he had changed the world for ever. He had brought an end to slavery.

With his victory complete the clouds began to turn grey. A sudden darkness was beginning to engulf the Coliseum. A lightning strike was seen. Then a second strike. Everyone in the Coliseum looked up, confused at what was going on. Out of nowhere a blistering stream of light came upon the Coliseum. It surrounded the whole huge building, then it narrowed down to focus on a spot in front of Femi. It was waiting for him to enter. With Femi's mission complete, he knew he had to return to his time. Femi began to approach the light, but before he could go Queen Amanirenas ran up to him and grabbed his hand.

She said, 'Where are you going? Stay with me and build a future with me! I can't do this without you.'

Femi turned around, placed one hand on her cheek and said 'I have to; this is not my time. I've completed my mission. On this journey I've seen and encountered things that I didn't expect to see. I've experienced emotions that I didn't know were possible. One thing I didn't expect was to fall in love. Amanirenas, I love you and will remember you always. But now I need you to go and rule your peoples, and make sure that what we started here lasts for many generations to come.'

Crying, she said, 'I will, I promise.'

For the final time Queen Amanirenas and Femi kissed passionately, then Femi walked towards the light. As he approached the light, the beads that had guided his travel suddenly reappeared. Normally they glowed to tell him where he would be heading next. This time, though, there was no glow.

'I guess the mission's truly finished,' Femi said to himself. He stepped into the light. He was content and maybe for the first time in his life genuinely happy. He had done what he had thought was impossible. He had eliminated slavery.

With a puff of smoke the light was gone from the sight of the people in the Coliseum, and with it Femi, beginning the journey back to his own time.

Chapter 28: A new world – for better or worse?

As Femi entered the light he found himself being whirled up in a thunderstorm, like when he had entered the time machine in the first place. As he swirled around in the mysterious cloud he could see elements of the journey that he had undertaken. He saw himself training on the west coast of Africa, he saw himself fighting the Portuguese, he witnessed himself rescuing Nat Turner, and he also witnessed himself killing Julius Caesar. Then all of a sudden he saw images of areas he hadn't been to. He saw spans of time that were different. He saw landmarks and major events that he had never seen or ever heard of. A new history was being written. Femi had completed his mission; he had eliminated slavery. The question now was: *what would the new world look like?*

Eventually the storm ended and he found himself crash-landing into a set of bins.

'Ouch, that was painful,' he said to himself. He got up and dusted himself down. He realised he was back in modern-day London. He was back in the alleyway where he had first met Mr Diggity.

'Mr Diggity!' he yelled. He yelled again but got no response.

For a moment he paused. He looked around at the surroundings. He knew he was back in London, but he felt that this was a different London. He smiled to himself and said, 'Right! Let's see what the world's like now that slavery doesn't exist.'

Femi wandered around the area that he used to know as Newham. He wandered around for hours and he started to realise this was very different from the London he had once known. In the Newham Femi had known he could be on the street and he would always find someone; very often he would bump into people that he knew. But now the streets were empty. The Newham he knew was no more. Instead of the hustle and bustle that once was Newham, now all Femi could see was emptiness, no people.

He said to himself, 'Hmmm, this isn't quite the world I'd expected.'

Eventually he came across a crumpled-up newspaper. He turned to the back to catch up on what had been happening in football; it was the norm for him to read a newspaper back to front. But to his surprise there was no football.

'No football, really? No Cristiano Ronaldo, Messi or Neymar? I wanted to rid the world of slavery. I didn't want football to disappear as well. Mr Diggity never warned me that was going to happen.'

And then as he leafed through the paper he noticed there was no mention of any sport whatsoever. He continued to look through the paper. Instead, there was one common theme that he *did* notice. There were no pictures of any white people. In fact there was no mention of anybody who wasn't black. When he got to the front of the paper he found the title quite interesting: *Poundered News: The Voice of the World.* Femi smiled. He had always wanted black people to have a stronger voice in world; now they had it.

Femi then spent some time walking through his neighbourhood. He came across the area he used to know as Upton Park. It had always been busy, especially on a Saturday when everyone was going to the market to get their groceries. But instead of the market all he saw was a wilderness.

'If Upton Park isn't here, where do people go to buy their groceries?' he thought to himself.

Another thought then occurred to him. In *Poundered News*, as well as not seeing any white people he hadn't seen any Indians. In fact Femi saw no mention of any other race. This sent a chill down his spine. He started to wonder, had his mission gone too far? He had wanted to end slavery. But he had never intended to eliminate all non-black races.

A sudden panic set in. As he continued to wander further into Newham not only did he see emptiness – he started to see devastation. He came across a series of rundown houses. It was as if his hometown had been besieged. Newham looked as if it had been caught up in a nuclear war. Mr Diggity had warned Femi that even though he could guarantee that slavery would be eliminated he would give Femi no promises about the world that he would come back to, and had warned that a heavy price might need to be paid. Femi was starting to wonder whether the price was too high.

Ridding the world of slavery had been supposed to make things better. It had been meant to create a world where black people would no longer suffer from racism and prejudice. The mission had been meant to enable Africa to blossom, as the continent would no longer be exploited for its resources, or its people be forced away from their homes to suffer a life of pain and misery. The mission had been meant to bring about a glorious new world order. But right now Femi was feeling that he might have doomed the world to an even more depressing existence. It seemed that his mission had resulted in one form of evil replacing another.

Femi saw an advertising board across the road: 'Hmm, some things never change. There are still people here in this world who'll try to sell you stuff regardless of what's going on.'

He decided to take a look at it, as he felt it might give him more insight into the new world he had entered. But what was on the board wasn't a product for sale. It was a man covered in battle armour. He wore a mask with bull horns pointing sideways. Femi also noticed an emblem, BLO, across the middle of the armour. He scrolled down the board and read *Black Lives Only*. He realised that this was the first significant consequence of the success of his mission. Instead of the institutionalised racism that had existed in the world he had come from, his mission had given rise to a new regime.

'Who *are* these guys?' Femi asked himself, worried. 'And more importantly, who's this guy with the bull horn helmet? What's so special about him?'

At that moment he heard footsteps. Unsure whose they were, he decided to take cover. He ran into one of the abandoned houses nearby. Whilst hiding behind the front door he discovered a crack in the door, enough to enable him to see who was approaching.

The footsteps got louder, and Femi realised what he was hearing was marching.

Soldiers dressed in the armour Femi had seen on the billboard appeared. They were shouting a chant: *'Black Lives Only, Black Lives Only, Black Lives Only!'*

Femi glanced up and down at the soldiers. He wanted to try to get some more intel about the new London that he had come back to. He spotted that the soldiers were all carrying flags with the Black Lives Only emblem.

As Femi inspected the flags more closely he made another shocking discovery. He saw that the flags had human heads on top of them. The heads weren't dummies; they were real human heads. Femi could see the blood still on some of them.

Despite the distance, he could smell the reek of death that these flags were carrying.

The heads were of non-black origin. Femi couldn't believe the new London he was witnessing: 'This is *barbaric*! What kind of horror is this? I wanted to save black people from slavery. I wanted to create a better world. Ok, my mission's created a world where black people are on top – but at what cost? Instead of being oppressed we're now the oppressors.'

Femi slumped down to his knees, his hands on top of his head, in disgust and despair. He was ashamed of the new world he had created, and softly moaned to himself, 'What have I done? *What have I done?*'

To be continued ...

Denis Olasehinde Akinmolasire

To Contact the Author:

www.akinsterbooks.co.uk

akinsterbooks@hotmail.com

https://m.facebook.com/akinsterbooks/

Twitter: lovewarandglory

Instagram: denisakinbookauthor